A
PROPHETIC
HISTORY

PART ONE

RICK JOYNER

MorningStar Publications

A DIVISION OF MORNINGSTAR FELLOWSHIP CHURCH

375 Star Light Drive, Fort Mill, SC 29715

A Prophetic History, Part I
by Rick Joyner
Copyright © 2009
Second Printing, 2010

Distributed by MorningStar Publications, Inc., a division of MorningStar
Fellowship Church, 375 Star Light Drive, Fort Mill, SC 29715

International Standard Book Number: 978-1-60708-294-1;
1-60708-294-2
MorningStar's website: www.MorningStarMinistries.org
For information call 1-800-542-0278

Cover design by Kevin Lepp
Book layout by Dana Zondory

Unless otherwise indicated, all Scripture quotations are taken from the
New American Standard Bible, copyright © 1960, 1962, 1963, 1968,
1971, 1973, 1974, 1977 by The Lockman Foundation. Italics in Scripture are for emphasis only.

TABLE OF CONTENTS

INTRODUCTION

This book is about a real journey and actual events with many witnesses—sometimes hundreds and even thousands. Even so, this is just the beginning of a story that is still unfolding. It was written to share experiences that have prophetic significance, not just because of what happened, but how. We see this prophesied in Scripture in Acts 2:17-18:

> **"And it shall be in the last days," God says, "that I will pour forth of My Spirit on all mankind; and your sons and your daughters shall prophesy, and your young men shall see visions, and your old men shall dream dreams;**
>
> **"even upon my bondslaves, both men and women, I will in those days pour forth of My Spirit and they shall prophesy."**

We see in **"the last days"** of this age that the Holy Spirit will be poured out upon God's bondservants, and the result of this will be dreams, visions, and prophecy. This is going to happen in **"the last days,"** because we will need this kind of guidance. The dreams, visions, and prophecies recorded here not only came to pass, but they did so in a way that we can expect to become increasingly common and normal for the Christian life.

We are living in the times when the supernatural is becoming natural, and the impossible is becoming probable. This truly is the greatest of all adventures and the most noble cause—the true Christian life. From the beginning, this has been the quest of those who have been associated with MorningStar churches and ministries. We have been a fellowship of those seeking to walk with God, believing that He is the same today as He was yesterday, that He has never changed, nor has He changed the way that He relates to and works through His people.

The word "history" was originally two words, *His* and *story*, meaning God's story. The Bible is a history book and was written to recount God's dealings with men to teach future generations the ways of God and the ways of men. True faith does not just believe all that was written in the Bible is true; rather, it is having the faith to see the same things happen in our own lives.

History is also written to record what we have learned in order to pass it on to future generations, so they don't have to learn many of the same lessons. However, few have grasped this great truth. The proverb, "Those who do not learn from history are doomed to repeat it," has been proven true over and over again. This is why the true prophets in Scripture, as well as in the church age, have been devoted students of history.

One primary way that history has accurately prophesied the future is that almost always every generation will make the same mistakes that the previous one made. The more the emerging generation says that they will be different—that they will not make the same mistakes, which almost every emerging generation asserts—the more definite it is that they will make the same mistakes. It will take the grace of God to be delivered from this deadly cycle. As James 4:6 declares, **"God is opposed to the proud, but gives grace to the humble."** Humility demands that we acknowledge we are not unlike our fathers and mothers, and that we need the grace of God to break this cycle. Humility also demands that we esteem and learn from what our fathers and mothers accomplished, which will always result in a devotion to understanding history.

Those who have that kind of humility can be trusted with one of the most valuable and powerful resources that one can have—a clear and accurate knowledge of the future, or prophecy. The church, and indeed the whole world, now stand in desperate need of this clear and accurate vision of the future. This need will grow more desperate with every passing year. Because the Lord has promised to freely give it to His people, it can turn the desperate life into a life of wonder, awe, and accomplishment.

This book is titled, *A Prophetic History,* because it has been just that. Most of the significant events and aspects of MorningStar were all prophesied and then fulfilled, often in the most unusual and unexpected ways. In some ways, it has seemed like one continuous thrill ride. As clearly as we have been shown many things before they happened, it still never ceases to amaze and surprise us when they do happen, mostly because of how they actually come to pass. This may have kept us on the edge of our seats, but it has also kept us interested. When I became a Christian I prayed for a life like this, but I think in every way it has been better and far more exciting than I ever expected. We know this is not because we are special, or because we in any way deserve it, but simply because we asked for it.

In this book and in the upcoming series, I am going to recount some of the highlights and lowlights of our history as a ministry. Each of our churches and every major aspect of our ministry have been built on a prophetic foundation, which means it was prophesied and then came to pass.

Our ministry may be unique. I know other works that have some prophetic foundations, but I'm not aware of any who have almost every aspect built on such a foundation. Why us? This may be because of our foolishness, lack of faith, or many other flaws, which required such extraordinary guidance. Even with such a clear course given to us, many times we have drifted from it. However, having a clear course helped us get back on track. We have been recipients of the great grace of God, and whatever has been accomplished, we sincerely can attribute to grace. I'm not saying this to be humble, but because it is true.

If we have had an attribute that has helped, I think it is because we have been blessed by having people join with us who just would not quit. We have also been joined by those who are comfortable in almost constant battle and controversy, since "spiritual bullets" are almost always buzzing around us. We have had our share of problems and made our share of mistakes, which are usually harder than external attacks, but rarely have we had anyone quit.

I am writing this for the purpose of honoring what the Lord has done, but also to help others who are about to make the uncommon, common—walking in a realm of miracles and wonder that ultimately exceeds anything that has been recorded before, even in Scripture. A generation is arising that will experience the **"greater works" (see John 14:12)**, which Jesus said would be done in His name because He has gone to the Father. This could be your prophetic destiny, the door which is opened through the expectation of faith.

We have known from the beginning that we are here to prepare the way for a greater ministry that is coming. Whether we are able to enter into this as Joshua and Caleb types remains to be seen. We have known that we are called to help prepare a generation who will walk in the greatest glory men have yet walked in on the earth, a life which Jesus demonstrated. As the church fathers have said, the Lord Jesus did not come to show us how God lived, but how we could live. The ultimate calling we each have is to be like Him and to do the works that He did. There will be a people who walk the earth and do this—demonstrating all that was gained for us through the New Covenant in Christ. It is our calling to help prepare the way for such a generation, and by this, prepare the way for the Lord to come back and take His dominion over the earth.

We prepare the way for the Lord by building a highway as we are told in Isaiah 40. Those who build highways must level the mountains and hills, and bring up the low places. They must cut through forests and jungles, and fill in swamps. Their progress can be slow, tedious, and dangerous. However, when they finish, others will be able to drive on their roads and zip along at 70 mph through the very places where before it may have recently taken a month to drive a mile. That's progress! We have benefited in this way from all who have gone before us, and we want to make the way easier and faster for those who come after us. This is our assignment. The ease at which others will be able to get to where we are will determine whether we have done our jobs well or not.

There are other reasons why the Lord has spoken to us so specifically and clearly about the building of our ministry. One is that we asked for it. We did not ask because we felt that we were good enough or wise enough, but because we felt we needed it. Though we may have had a specific calling that required this in some ways, I do not think we have received anything that is not available to any one of His people who asked Him for it. Therefore, another basic purpose of this book is not to marvel at what has been done, but if something inspires you, ask for it, seek for it, and keep asking and seeking until the door is opened.

MorningStar has gathered those who love the prophetic, and we ask for it, just as the Scriptures encourage us to do. Even so, we have also learned an important prophetic principle—the more clearly and specifically the

Lord speaks about something, it is usually an indication of how difficult it will be. Therefore, we have also learned to be happy when He is not speaking to us with such clarity, knowing this usually means we will have a time of relative ease for a while. Even the best soldiers cannot endure constant battle without some rest. We have learned to embrace the times of rest as being the great blessings that they are, but to also be ready when we hear the trumpet call. When the Lord starts speaking to us clearly, we have learned to check our armor because we know we will be returning into the fight.

Every life on earth will have hardships. As the saying goes, "Life is hard, and then you die." I think we could change that to, "Life is hard if you do not learn to die daily." If we have died with Christ and are dead to this world, what can the world do to us? Those who live the crucified life are the most alive of all and probably have the most joyous lives of all. Those who are Christ's slaves are the most free of all. When we live like this, which He said His disciples would do, we can say, "Life is hard, but then we live—forever!"

Even so, as inferred above, we know a major reason why the Lord has spoken to us clearly so many times is because of our lack of faith, lack of courage, or lack of wisdom. I have been rebuked numerous times for being slow of hearing and dull in my understanding, which required the Lord to speak to me loudly and clearly. Some of the greatest things I've experienced were not because of my faith, but because of a lack of it. However, I have continually asked the Lord to help me in my unbelief, and He has been very faithful to answer that prayer.

I am writing this to pass on some lessons that can be valuable for the future. Acts 2:17-18 makes it clear that **"in the last days"** the Spirit will be poured out, and the result of this will be prophecy and prophetic revelation through dreams and visions. As we get closer to the consummation of this age, prophecy will increase, which is one of the major signs of the times. However, it is not coming just as a sign of the times, but because we are going to need very clear guidance to accomplish our purposes in these times.

In the times that are quickly coming upon us, the church that does not have a trustworthy prophetic ministry will not make it. The prophets are the eyes of the body, and those who try to continue walking blindly will simply not survive the increasing difficulties. Yet we have the great promise in Proverbs 4:18, **"But the path of the righteous is like the light of dawn, that shines brighter and brighter until the full day."** If we are on **"the path of the righteous,"** or the right path, the path will get clearer and brighter as we walk. Those who are on the right path do not fear the darkness because their light will always be increasing.

The path we have been on to see authentic prophetic ministry restored to the church has been getting clearer. MorningStar has been a gathering place for prophetic people and for those who have the hearts of spiritual pioneers, which I count among some of our greatest blessings. Because of this, many who join with us only come for a time to get what they need for their own journeys and then move on. We always miss them, but we are here to help true sojourners. Spiritual pioneers are usually not content with abiding in the same place for very long. They have to keep moving on and pressing the envelope. Therefore, we know that some of the great friends who come to be with us, "come to pass" through. Even so, great joy comes from hearing about their exploits.

One reason it has taken me so long to write this book is because I also do not like looking back, but rather pressing forward. However, as I have begun to recount our history, I know how much I need to be reminded of many of these lessons. Just as all explorers or pioneers have probably wandered into a few box canyons, which forced them to do some backtracking, we have done the same. We can show you many things that can make your way easier and some ways to avoid, which can save you a lot of time and resources. For years, we used to say the most common word around MorningStar was "oops!" I have personally made quite a few costly leadership mistakes, some after neglecting clear prophetic warnings. I would be happy for you to learn from my mistakes and not make the same ones.

If you are a true prophet or spiritual pioneer, you will be both battle-hardened and battle-scarred. We have also experienced spectacular victories, some much bigger and greater than we expected. I would be very happy for you to have even greater ones, because the church needs more and greater victories to accomplish her purpose for these times. For this reason, I have been selective in this history and only included the accounts that have important and timely lessons. I will try to tell this history the way it actually happened to the degree that this is possible, being a subjective witness and one who looks so far forward that I have a greatly underdeveloped memory.

I also know we **"see in part,"** and **"know in part" (see I Corinthians 13:9).** Those who walked through the things that you are about to read, even walking through them right next to me, may remember them differently in some ways, and we can both be right. We actually see truth in the way that the four Gospels tell the same events from different perspectives. The four together give us a much more complete and accurate picture. The details of these Gospels do not conflict with each other but complement each other.

Every history is written subjectively, regardless of how objective the author claims to be. However, God records history completely and accurately in "The Books of Life." On that great Judgment Day, every perspective on every history will be settled. Even so, my goal is for this to be "His-story" or His perspective, not just mine. I seek the anointing, perspective, and articulation of the Holy Spirit, asking to see with His eyes and understand with His heart. At the same time, I know that I only see and know in part. Being a part of this history, I may not be able to claim objectivity, but that does not mean my subjective view does not have value or is inaccurate.

I am sure that some of the lessons we have learned, or are learning, will be crucial for the church's survival in the times to come, because that has been told to me over and over. However, our goal is not just survival, but the triumph of the truth that the church is called to experience and be.

So, strap on your seatbelt and get ready. It will be an interesting ride. At times, you will likely be thrilled and inspired, and at other times, you may question whether you want to walk down a similar path. That is understandable, but the best path has already been chosen for you. This can help you see it much more clearly and walk down it more easily than we did at times. We are happy about that, and it makes even our most costly experiences worth it.

The people who I am writing about in this account are real people, and I will use their real names, unless I state otherwise. Most are still alive. The places are real and can be visited. However, this is not written so you can relive our story, but rather to encourage you to make your own.

CHAPTER ONE
THE JOURNEY BEGINS

Because I am the founder and the Executive Director of MorningStar, I will start with a brief history of my own life. This book is not about me, and I will only share the parts that are relative to this history.

I had such a profound supernatural conversion experience that I do not think I have ever doubted the reality of God since that day. On the day that I was born again, I was also introduced to the power of personal prophecy. Because of this, I immediately understood what Paul wrote in I Timothy 1:18-19: **"This command I entrust to you, Timothy, my son, in accordance with the prophecies previously made concerning you, that by them you fight the good fight, keeping faith and a good conscience."** I have been kept in the Lord, and at least a few times, my life was saved by the power of personal prophecy. This is one reason why I am committed to seeing authentic prophetic ministry restored to the church in our times. I have seen many Christians, churches, and ministries lost that could have been saved if they had been open to direct guidance from the Lord through His prophets. This continues to motivate me and many others to see authentic prophetic ministry restored to the church, and take the place that the Lord and His Scriptures give it.

From the beginning of my Christian life, people have called me a prophet. I don't think I have ever called myself one. Julie and I have been married for more than thirty years, and she says that she has never heard me call myself a prophet either. I have had many prophetic experiences, and I have a pretty good track record for what I have prophesied coming to pass, but I think there is more to being a prophet than that. I also see in the New Testament that what we are supposed to be experiencing in the New Covenant should be greater than what was experienced under the Old Testament. I don't see that yet, and I do not want to dilute the value of our spiritual currency by calling it something that does not yet measure up. I get chided and rebuked for this stand, but it remains my stand.

Even so, from my earliest days as a Christian I have loved the prophetic gifts, prophetic ministries, prophetic experiences, and prophetic people. I know they are a weird and difficult lot, but I love them and feel more comfortable around them than any others. I have learned to understand and trust them. I have therefore always gravitated toward them, and to some degree at least, they seem to gravitate to me. I count this as one of my greatest blessings.

I also confess to not having much patience with pseudo-prophets and pretenders. Many of these have greatly clouded the waters and made the way much more difficult for the real prophets who are rising. Even so, it seems that one of the primary tests that the real seed must endure is growing up together with the tares. I have repeatedly witnessed those who reject the real while almost constantly being taken in by the false. Then they blame all prophetic people. For this reason, being called a prophet in our times has often been more of an accusation than an honor, making you a bigger target. Indeed, it seems that almost no prophets are honored in their own time, but after they're dead everyone wants to honor them because they are no longer a threat. Even so, all of this helps to purify the true and drive away many who are just seeking their own recognition through such a ministry.

In spite of all the pitfalls and problems, being around authentic prophetic people is one of the most exciting things you can experience in this life. In my first couple of years as a Christian, I was privileged to meet and develop relationships with some who had authentic prophetic gifts. I witnessed their value and impact. I was the recipient of prophecies through them that helped set my course and keep me on track. Some of these were so spectacular that I was in continual awe and wonder of the Lord and His people. I fell in love with the church with a passion that I had never had for anything else before. I could not believe that I was part of such a dynamic force in the earth, and I could not understand why anything so dynamic had not yet taken over the earth!

I had a lot to learn, of course, but I still see the body of Christ, overall, as the most wonderful, powerful, and successful entity on the planet, even though I know it is still only operating at a fraction, probably less than 10 percent of its true potential and ability. When the body of Christ stands up to become all that she is called to be, the whole earth and both heaven and hell will without a doubt take notice. Nothing in history will have been as exciting as this will be, but the preparation for it calls for a lot of faith, patience, and endurance that not many seem to have. Even so, it will happen. It is written, and it will come to pass.

When I was thrust into full-time ministry, I had been a Christian for barely two years. I took comfort in the Book of Acts when Paul appointed elders in the new churches that seemed to be even much younger in the Lord than I was. Even so, I was a very poor pastor. In fact, I was the worst pastor I have ever heard of, and I think I wounded far more of God's people than I helped during those early days. That is probably why not many pastors and churches want prophetic people around, at least not until they are mature. There is a spiritual principle that anything which comes too easily or too quickly is usually insignificant. If you want to be a part of something truly significant, you will have to pay a price for it.

Even so, I confess that if I came through our church doors right now as I was then I would not be happy about it! My consolation and hope is based on how miserably Moses also failed the first time he sought to serve God's people. This is not to in any way imply that I have a ministry like his, but that I failed the first time just like him. I had to spend a lot of time in the wilderness pondering how inadequate I was for what I was called to do.

Even though I was so young and foolish in the Lord, my ministry and influence grew for a time. Soon I was asked to speak in other churches and then at conferences. I was quite determined to be another Apostle Paul, and deep in my heart, I probably thought I could surpass him! Of course, there was a lot of selfish ambition and pride mixed in this vision, but also a love for the church and a desire to see her become all that she was called to be. Because of my supernatural experience in coming to the Lord, I felt that true church life should be everything that was experienced by the church in the first century. I had some spectacular experiences in my life that caused a number of people to want to be near me, even though it could be dangerous.

However, as stated, I also had some spectacular failures. For a time, we had a fellowship that was bonded together like no other I had seen at the time. Then I was shown that it was built more on me than on the Lord. I had not laid the right foundation, and I was devastated—so devastated that I overreacted. I now know that the Lord just wanted to bring some correction before we became seriously off track, but I was so appalled at myself that I felt I had to leave the ministry, and I did. This too was self-will and sort of a reverse pride where I thought I had to fix myself before God could really use me.

Of course, He also knew that I would overreact. He helped steer my course and richly blessed me, even when I had departed from His will in some basic ways. I thank Him for this, and learned that He will always bless His children as much as He can; however, He will bless many things He will not inhabit. If you want more than just His blessings and if you want Him, you must obey and follow Him.

I had been a part-time flight instructor and corporate pilot while I was in ministry in the early days. When I felt I needed to leave the ministry, I took a full-time job flying corporate aircrafts in Mississippi, far away from my failures. I loved flying, and with any flying job, you often spend many hours a day waiting in airports or hotel rooms, which I used to study and seek to know God better. I was stripped of any feeling that I deserved to be a leader in the church, and I didn't really care about that anymore. The greatest desire of my life was to know God. This was a perfect situation for that, and I was very happy. One of my greatest joys has been learning and studying, and I was again able to spend most of my time doing this. Then, one day I had a vision that I knew would be a focus for the rest of my life.

Teaching Center/Prophetic Community

My vision for a "prophetic community" began in 1980. In spite of my poor leadership, our church in North Carolina had touched on a type of fellowship that I began to miss very much and could not find in any other church. I met some wonderful people during that time who would have a great impact on my life, but it was not really a bonding around church life as much as it was outside of it. I had been shown at the beginning of my Christian walk that I would be limited in my spiritual maturity and the ability to fulfill my purpose without a strong and vital local church life. Therefore, I resolved to always be vitally engaged in local church life, but I could not find the depth of church life that I was seeking.

I began to inquire of the Lord about why what I felt to be essential was hard to find anywhere in the church. Most of the ministry I witnessed seemed to promote superficiality in church relations and a distance between the leadership and the people that seemed counterproductive to building a strong church. Then Julie and I found a little church headed by an orthopedic surgeon, Dr. Jim Hughes. In fellowship and relationships, this church was wonderful. They did not understand many things that I was seeking, like the prophetic, but they embraced us warmly, and they were such great people that we were very happy there. I might have been content there for the rest of my life, but the Lord had other plans.

I was given a vision of what the church would become. As wonderful as our little fellowship was, we were not at all what I was shown, which was a force in the earth that shook the powers of heaven and hell. I was also shown much of what would be required to attain to this. It began a drive in me where I could not be content without it. I was also shown that the foundation of such a powerful church would require prophets and teachers who had learned to worship the Lord together like they did at Antioch. I was told that the Lord could not release true apostolic authority to the church again until this happened. I was then shown a community where both prophets and teachers would live together, loving and esteeming one another, and would learn to serve the Lord together. I was also given a promise that true apostolic ministry was going to be restored to the church and that this community would have a part in it.

I was so captivated by what I had seen that I could hardly think of anything else. However, I was still stinging from my own previous failures as a leader, and I never considered that I was capable of leading such a movement. I would have been content to just be one of the prophets or teachers, but I desperately wanted to see it come to pass.

It was at about this time that my corporate flying job ended, and Doc Hughes (as I called him) suggested that we start a small aircraft charter business together. He bought an airplane, I walked everything through the FAA to get our charter, and sought enough business to make a living. The business became successful and grew quickly, becoming quite large. I bought Doc Hughes out because it was my nature to move much faster than it was his. Looking back, I am sorry that I did not slow down and was not more willing to go at his pace, but that is how we often learn—the hard way! Before I knew it, I had dozens of people working for me. I was making a lot of money, but I had very little time for the Lord or my studies. I continued to fly, mostly so I would have hours for praying and thinking, away from phones and the constant questions of employees and customers.

As exciting and profitable as my business became, for some reason I was getting emptier rather than more fulfilled. Because of my previous failure, for a time I enjoyed the respect that came with success. Even powerful business people and politicians wanted to know me. The attention was nice, but it soon became obvious that with such respect and attention came demands for my time and my resources. I thoroughly enjoyed some of these friends, but even the deepest relationships were superficial, and deep down they were all about what we could do for each other in other superficial endeavors. Without question, church life and friendship among ministers can be very much the same—unless there is one factor: the awesome manifest presence of the Lord. When the Lord is in our midst, it cannot help but to be about Him and not us.

Two Trees

It was during this time that I wrote my first book, *There Were Two Trees in the Garden.* While it was being edited, I was alarmed by how a publisher had changed some of the statements in it to fit better with their doctrines, so I decided to self-publish rather than have the message changed. I formed a 501c3 organization so I could do this as a ministry rather than as a business, thinking this too would help keep the message more pure. I named the ministry MorningStar after the title given to Jesus in the Book of Revelation (see Revelation 22:16). MorningStar is one of my favorite names for Him because I felt that I was called to live in a time that would see the dawning of His day.

I personally paid for the first printing of *Two Trees* and gave them away, refusing to take money for them simply because I was doing so well financially that I wanted them to be gifts. After the first shipment of books was delivered, I heard the Spirit speak to me and say that MorningStar was going to be much bigger than my aviation business.

At that time, my business had more than sixty mechanics at our base airport, numerous pilots and support personnel, dozens of aircrafts in our charter department, a flight school, aircraft sales, and more than one hundred other aircrafts based with us, making our airport, which I leased from the county, the busiest in the state. I could not comprehend how MorningStar could ever become bigger than that, and at the time, I had no vision for MorningStar other than publishing and distributing a few Christian books. However, the Lord had spoken this so clearly, I could not deny it.

I had five thousand copies of *Two Trees* printed and expected that to be a lifetime supply. I only gave them away, and made no attempt to get them in bookstores or other outlets. However, gradually requests started to increase for them, but not so much that I felt I would ever exhaust the first printing. I really had no idea that it would soon be a bestseller around the world.

The Call

As the fulfillment and excitement of the business waned, I became determined to build the community I had seen. Like the movie, *Field of Dreams,* I thought that if I built it, the people would come. I bought some property and Julie and I began having the main house remodeled. I also began to work on clearing the land and shaping it.

That's when I fell in love with tractors and earth-moving equipment, and more than anything—the land itself. I began to feel like every tree was a personal friend, and I loved the animals that lived on the land. I became convinced that the mandate given to Adam to "cultivate the land" (see Genesis 2:15) was still a deep call within us. One day while I was working and thanking the Lord for that beautiful land, I heard Him say that it was indeed good land, but it was not the place that He had chosen for the community He had shown me. I was stunned.

Then the Lord began to speak to me about my presumption in determining to build this community from my own resources so that I could say that I had built it without offerings. This had offended Him, and He said, "Don't you think that I can provide for My own purposes?"

When I was shown the depth of my pride and presumption, I was shaken, just like I had been when I had seen how far off my ministry had been before. He then said that He was going to use me to help establish the community that He had shown me and the coming prophetic and apostolic ministries. He began speaking to me about returning to North Carolina, and specifically to "the mountains of North Carolina."

However, I was feeling like such a failure that I had a hard time thinking about going back into ministry, but I did have a deep yearning for it. I had accomplished my dream of being a professional pilot and building a successful business. By my standards I had become quite well off, but was still empty. Nothing else could ever be as fulfilling for me as being in the ministry and building people, not just things. He assured me that this was my calling, and that my failures would help me to understand how much I had to learn about waiting and abiding in Him. He also showed me that I would have to put my business on the altar and return to living by faith in His provision.

This is not to imply that using our own resources to do things for the kingdom is wrong, but I was doing it in pride, which the Lord would build nothing on. I asked the Lord to do whatever it took for me to become useful to Him. Within thirty days, my aviation business, which had been thriving and growing, crashed. Soon I was in bankruptcy. I was able to give the property that I had purchased, along with our dream home, back to the bank in exchange for our debts. I sold all of my planes and other assets and was left with a net worth that I computed to be very close to zero. About the only thing I had left was a word from the Lord to "go to the mountains of North Carolina."

A few months later, we left Mississippi with exactly what we had come with—a car and about two thousand dollars. However, I had a great deal of experience and two daughters, Anna who was three and Aaryn who was one. They were an incredible joy, but also an incredible responsibility. I had made and lost a fortune, but when we headed for North Carolina, I had more peace and joy in my life than I had known for years. I knew I was in the Lord's will.

My vision had actually grown stronger through all of my troubles with the business. I was more excited about building the community I had been shown than I had ever been about building a business. I almost felt like I was born again, again. When I had worked as a pilot, I used to say that the sky was my office, and now I felt that it was in an even greater way. I felt that the Lord had made the heavens so big just to remind us that in Him there are no limits to how high we can go! As much as I loved airplanes and flying jets, this was much, much better.

I did not know exactly what I was going to do, how I was going to support my family, or build the community. I felt like Abraham leaving Ur; I really did not know where I was going, but I did know what I was looking for—what God was building, the city which has foundations. It was both exhilarating and scary.

SPYING OUT THE LAND

Just before leaving Mississippi, I took a two-week ministry trip to visit some people in Georgia, North Carolina, and Virginia that I had known when I was in ministry before, as well as a couple of churches that had asked me to come speak to them after they had received a copy of *Two Trees*. I also was hoping to gain a perspective of the present state of the church and to be led to the place where the community I had seen was to be built. What I witnessed was a church in such a visionless, purposeless state that I was almost cast into despair (this was in 1987). I returned from this trip grieved by everything I had seen. I learned in business that to succeed you had to "buy low and sell high," and I was certainly going to be investing in the church when it was low.

That first trip also cost me money. The honorariums did not even cover my expenses, which was discouraging because I had no other source of income. I had been through faith tests before, but I started to sense this was going to be a big one. It was, but for a very short time. In just a few months, I would be living better than I ever had, while making less than I probably ever had. The Lord had everything planned, as He always does.

However, the trip had not been encouraging, and I did not find the land for the community either. Harry and Louise Bizzell had invited me to bring my family up to their retreat center just south of Charlotte, North Carolina. They had a small cabin for us to stay in until I found the place where I was to go. I inquired of the Lord about this, and He only said that He was going to bless us in the city and in the country. This was the first indication that we might have to stay in Charlotte a little longer than I had considered and that we might even have some kind of destiny there too.

Julie and I loved Harry and Louise. The little cabin that they offered for us to live in was a fraction of the size of our dream home we had just left, but I was much happier and had much more peace than I had known for years. I think Julie was too, though she had become quite jaded toward me and my visions after the loss of our business and home. This was understandable.

When we moved to the little cabin, I was also very excited at the prospect of spending some time with Harry and Louise, since they were two of the finest and most interesting people that I knew. They also had a love for each other that was infectious, which was badly needed for Julie and I at the time.

I also remained deeply troubled by what I felt the Lord had shown me about the state of the church. As I quickly learned, much of the despair that the church had fallen into was the result of another Christian community that had been just a couple of miles from Harry and Louise's home—the fall of PTL, or Heritage USA.

I had only a superficial understanding of what PTL had been about and had never connected with it. I did not have even the slightest thought that somehow my destiny would be connected with this, and that Jim Bakker, whose failure I could well identify with, would one day be a great friend. I also had little concept of how the wildness, weirdness, and magnificence was all about to ratchet up dramatically.

CHAPTER TWO
A VISION OF THE HARVEST

When I returned home to prepare for our move to Charlotte, I went to my study to do some paperwork and to pray over all that I was feeling from my trip, especially about the low state of the church. I was immediately caught up into a prophetic experience like I had never had before. For two-and-a half-days, I was shown a panorama of things to come in extraordinary detail like I had never seen before. When it was over, I tried to write it down, but I felt that it could take me years to remember it all. I felt that this encounter would set the course for the rest of my life. I was right.

This vision also changed my view of the church, the state that it was in, and what was about to happen. I went from deep discouragement to great hope. I could not wait to get on with the job I was called to do, whatever that might be. I saw victory, hope, expectation, and good things in the same people that I had recently felt negatively about.

I was so changed in my perspective that I thought I had been given a new set of eyes to see through.

To this day, I am regularly told that I am too optimistic about people and not discerning enough, and in some cases I'm sure this is true. However, I was not previously that way. At the time I had this vision, I had just been betrayed by friends whom I had done a lot for, and it had cost me a business I had labored greatly to build, which was to me a large fortune. Just before that, I had received the worst personal attack from close Christian friends. I had become jaded and distrustful toward people, and suddenly everything that had happened to me seemed petty and easy to overlook. I started seeing even feeble Christians as potential spiritual giants who could change nations.

Granted, I have been deceived by people that I put a lot of trust in and used by those who I believed when they said they came to help me. However, I would rather be taken advantage of occasionally than lose the gift that I think this visitation gave me to see people, especially the church, in the best light. I want to see them as they are called to be, not as they may be presently. If I have been called as a prophet, I pray for the prophetic gift that Ezekiel had. He was able to see in dry bones an exceedingly great army, and he prophesied life to those bones until they became what they were called to be (see Ezekiel 37). That is the prophetic gift I pray for more than any other.

I wrote a brief summary of this vision which I titled, *A Vision of the Harvest,* and sent it to the two hundred people on our mailing list, which was mostly our Christmas card list. Within weeks, this vision was lighting a fire in many. Churches and ministries, big and small, from everywhere it seemed, started asking for permission to reprint it. Within weeks, I was receiving letters and requests to minister from all over the world. Some had called it the most widely-distributed prophetic word in modern times. I think it made its way into every country on the earth.

Even though this vision had the same impact on me, lighting a fire that I felt would carry me the rest of my life, I was shocked by how quickly it had spread, and it kept increasing. I could barely answer the requests for ministry, much less go to them all. As more national and international ministries printed and distributed the vision, the fire was fanned even more.

As I looked at the requests for me to speak, I was a bit concerned because it had been so long since I had spoken publically that I felt I would probably be a disappointment wherever I went. Even so, I was called to go, and so I did. I think I was a disappointment to many, who almost always wanted me to prophesy, especially about them and their purposes. I was far more devoted to teaching, which I felt they needed in order to fulfill their purposes. I was not like the typical Pentecostal or Charismatic prophet, but I sought to give prophetic teachings and messages that related to the purposes of God for those to whom I was speaking. The teachings were also practical and called for practical action. Some grasped what I was doing and embraced it, but I was never under the delusion that all did. Even so, I was resolved to be who I had been called to be and not what people wanted me to be. I was not lacking for places to go, so I think this was grace from God to help me not to compromise.

The Prophets Are Coming

It was at about this same time that the Lord began to show me that it was time to restore the prophetic ministry to the church and that it would eventually mature into something more extraordinary than the world had ever witnessed, even in the Old Testament. I was also shown that this was only preparation for the restoration of the apostolic ministry that was to follow.

I was told that I would soon meet some of His prophets and teachers. He said that there were already some who walked in a high level of prophetic authority and were laying the foundation for what was to come. Within weeks of this, I began meeting people who daily walked in a level of revelation and supernatural ministry like I had never personally witnessed or even heard of before. Even so, they too had a vision for something that was coming which was much more than any of us had ever witnessed. We all seemed to have a part of the same picture—there was a church life coming that would be like a last-day Book of Acts, only better.

The Christian life is supposed to be the greatest and most fulfilling adventure that a person can experience, but it seems that very few have such a life. However, at the time most Christians seemed to be mired in such deep boredom that only a fear of hell could keep them in it. It was hard to even find those who were compelled by a love for God, much less His people. Even so, that year I began a journey that would be what I believed in my heart to be a taste of the way the true Christian life is supposed to be.

Many had longed to see the Book of Acts become the standard of church life again, but at times over the next few years I would think that what was happening was indeed better than the Book of Acts. It would fade a bit and then plateau. Another wave would come, and then another plateau. This was repeated over and over. As they kept coming, the waves seemed to get bigger and the plateaus were shorter. We soon began to recognize the pattern of birth pangs, or contractions, and knew something in the Spirit was about to be birthed.

This is a pattern that continues with almost every move of God. During this period, we saw works of God and had many prophetic experiences that surpassed any expectations I had. We were also told repeatedly that we had not even begun to experience all that the Lord was going to do in these last days, and we were still just laying a foundation for it. Adventure is about to be returned to the church, and all Christians will continually be in awe at the great things that the Lord is doing. Everything that we are doing now as a ministry is devoted to preparing the way for what is coming. The Lord really has saved His best wine for last!

The following are just some of the people I met during this period who I was shown had helped, or would help, lay a foundation for the last-day ministry of the church.

Leonard Ravenhill

It was soon after I had received *A Vision of the Harvest* and as we were preparing for our move to North Carolina, that I received a call from Joyce Green, wife of the late Milton Green. Milton had just passed away and Joyce asked me to speak at their annual conference in his place, which was held in Palestine, Texas. I agreed to do this. While I was speaking at one of the meetings, I noticed an elderly man come in with a small group and sit in the back. I knew right away that there was an extraordinary anointing on this man. As I looked at him, the Holy Spirit spoke to me saying, "He is a modern 'Simeon.' He too serves night and day in prayer while waiting for the last-day harvest. Like Simeon, he will be allowed to see the salvation of the Lord in its infancy."

I was so taken with this word that immediately after my message, I went to meet this man and share the word that I had just been given for him. His name was Leonard Ravenhill, one of the classic writers of our time, and one of the great prophetic voices of the twentieth century. I was inspired by our short time together that day, and we agreed to stay in touch, which we did. This was more of a divine encounter than I realized at the time, which led to a significant prophetic event that I will describe later. His words to me would add much fire to the vision I had.

Leonard Ravenhill started writing to me frequently, and I treasured his letters greatly, but I don't think I could read a single one. I don't know how the postman read the address on some of them. For years to come, I visited

Leonard when I could, and he became, and remains, a great inspiration to me. Later, I introduced Leonard to Mike Bickle and then John Wimber, which set off some truly historic events we will discuss later.

James Robison

It was also at this time that James Robison asked for my permission to print *A Vision of the Harvest* in his magazine, *Restoration*. A few weeks later while passing through Texas, I met with James, and he asked me to do a few television programs with him. This led James to read the only book I had written at the time, *There Were Two Trees in the Garden.* James is not only one of the most anointed evangelists of our time, but because of his uncommon depth of passion and devotion, he is also one of the most anointed spiritual promoters of our time. James liked *Two Trees* so much that he asked to print a special edition and took one of his entire programs just to read quotes from it. Combined with the printing of my vision in his magazine, our little ministry was quickly catapulted into such visibility in the body of Christ that orders for books and invitations for me to speak at churches and conferences were coming in from around the world like a tidal wave.

One day when I was sitting in James' office talking, he told me about a former Dallas Theological Seminary professor who had just been fired for embracing the present operation of the gifts of the Spirit. While James was telling me about him, I heard the Lord as if He were speaking in my other ear, saying, "You will meet Jack Deere. He will be one of My most important teachers in the last days." That obviously got my attention, so I was determined to meet this man. I had no idea that it had already been arranged in a most unusual manner, which is kind of a hallmark of the Lord.

James Robison was one of the most clear and powerful prophetic voices in the church for a time. He has since entered into a special season of sinking his roots deeper and has been called to enjoy the Lord and His people. However, he will again stand up to prophesy clear direction and purpose that will mobilize many of God's people and turn many others to the Lord.

A Gathering of Seekers

Soon after we had moved to The Lamb's Chapel, the Christian retreat center overseen by the Bizzells, I was asked to attend a small gathering of prophetic people in Minneapolis, hosted by Chuck Porta and Jim McCrackin. I think the only person attending that I knew was Art Katz, and I was looking forward to seeing him again. However, I had a great sense of a unique destiny on this meeting that went beyond just seeing an old friend.

The gathering itself seemed unremarkable to be a gathering of prophets, which it was called, but in truth I think it was a gathering of prophetically-oriented people who were true seekers of God. I felt a strong bond to several people who I met there, including Carlton Kenney, and three men from Kansas City—Mike Bickle, Noel Alexander, and Jim Goll.

During the meetings, Mike told me about some of his experiences with a prophetic man in Kansas City named Bob Jones. I was amazed and very interested by these accounts. When I asked Mike if I could meet Bob, he not only said that I could, but he knew that I was supposed to meet him. He said that Bob already knew about me from some dreams that he had received. He also said that Bob had talked for years about two men from North Carolina they were supposed to meet, and when my *Vision of the Harvest* had come to them, they knew I was one of them. My interest in meeting Bob was perked up even more.

Even though Mike was young when this meeting took place, I felt that he displayed leadership abilities far beyond his years. It was not common to see someone with such zeal for the Lord who also had depth and wisdom. I felt immediately that Mike was not here to just prepare the way for what was to come but to be a part of what was to come and to be a great leader in it. I have since watched Mike go through many things, but I have never lost this confidence in his ultimate purpose.

BOB JONES

A few weeks later, Mike came to North Carolina with Bob and Viola Jones, and to my astonishment, they brought Jack Deere with them. The next couple of days were even more extraordinary than I had hoped. I was driving Mike, Bob, and Jack to The Lamb's Chapel Retreat Center, and as we got close, Bob started saying, "I was here last night!" He accurately described some of the features of the retreat center that we were still a few miles away from. He then started describing Harry Bizzell who I was taking them to meet but had not told them anything about.

When we were walking to the house, one of the Bizzell's daughters was leaving. Bob stopped her and told her a few details about her life. Visibly stunned and weeping, she followed us back into the house. Before I had finished the introductions to Harry and Louise, Bob said that he already knew about them (because of his dreams) and started telling them things about their lives, of which I was not even aware. I had never seen Harry cry before, but in just a couple of minutes, the tears were flowing.

I had seen a lot of personal prophecy before, but never anything with the kind of depth and accuracy that Bob walked in. What was even more amazing to me was that he seemingly walked in it all of the time. He would even look at things, such as trees, and tell what had happened to them recently or what was about to happen to them, like being hit with a disease. When I had the opportunity to check these things out, they always proved accurate. This awakened in me a much greater appreciation for the power of personal prophetic ministry than I ever had before.

I also felt supernaturally bonded to Mike Bickle and Jack Deere, which continues to this day. Mike was one of the most passionate lovers of God that I had met, and Jack, in spite of all of his great academic learning, was one of the most spiritually hungry and teachable people I had met. I was also told at that time that all of us would work together for the purposes of the Lord.

Hurricane Hugo

After the extraordinary afternoon with the Bizzells, we were standing in the parking lot at The Lamb's Chapel getting ready to leave, when Bob started talking about seeing a great wind coming, and how it was so strong that he saw the rain blowing horizontally. We both speculated that this was something spiritual, but it was obviously significant, even if a bit obscure. I went to Kansas City to visit the Kansas City Fellowship, and as soon as Bob saw me, he started talking about how he had seen more concerning the wind that would come against us in Charlotte. He said he had seen in a vision a great demon coming up out of the sea and turning into a hurricane, and it came to Charlotte.

Because no hurricane had ever come that far inland before (more than two hundred miles), I did not think that this could be literal but rather spiritual, and I asked Bob if he thought it was meant spiritually. He did not know, but just felt an urgency to share with me what he had seen.

Bob also saw trees being flattened all around our property in North Carolina. This should have given us the hint that this was literal, but again, no hurricane had ever come close to going that far inland before. That this was literal seemed out of the realm of possibility, so we spiritualized it or concluded that this had a spiritual application, not a physical one. I had basically concluded that the winds represented a great move of the Spirit, which is sometimes represented in Scripture as a wind, and that this would be disruptive to all who did not have strong roots, and so forth.

Bob tended to agree with these thoughts. As I would learn well, prophetic people can be just as dull as anyone else when it comes to understanding what the Lord is saying. Even if a prophet is receiving a clear word or revelation, because we see in part, know in part, and "prophesy in part," the most any prophetic person is going to receive will be only part of the revelation. To get the whole picture, we must put the part we have been given together with what others are seeing. This remains one of the weakest links in the prophetic movement—the failure of prophetic people to link together and share their parts with each other to get the whole picture.

In the meantime, Charlotte had been awarded a National Basketball Association (NBA) team, which they named the Charlotte Hornets. They named their mascot "Hugo the Hornet," which was just a few months before Hurricane Hugo was to strike Charlotte. This was to be an important part of the revelation, which became clear after the storm, but it would have been hard to relate all of this as it was unfolding. That, too, is important to understand about prophecy. Many people want to use prophecy as proof of the Lord's existence or interest in the affairs of men. However, I think it is rarely given to prove Himself but rather simply to give understanding of His ways and His acts to those who already believe Him, which usually does not come together until after the events prophesied have happened.

This has been a bit of a recurring theme throughout our prophetic journey. We have matured somewhat so that we do not immediately tend to spiritualize what the Lord says to us, but we have at the same time become even more humbled by our own fumbling and understanding. Regardless of how much we are shown, it is still only part of the picture. Even though we may only see in part, it can still be useful, and at times incredibly helpful. It also serves to keep us humble and teachable.

It was at about this same time that I was asked to share with a number of church leaders at the home of one of Charlotte's leading citizens. I knew they were going to ask me what I saw the principality over Charlotte to be, and I had been shown a great deal about this in the preceding months. What I had seen was called "charismatic witchcraft," which has nothing to do with the Charismatic movement, but rather a form of witchcraft that has its roots in human charisma. Witchcraft is basically counterfeit spiritual authority, which uses manipulation, control, and other forms of influence to control and manipulate in place of the Holy Spirit. This is a form of counterfeit spiritual authority that often gains entry into churches, movements, and as I had been shown, was a major factor in bringing down the PTL ministry that Charlotte was still reeling from.

I went to this meeting with the church leaders with the purpose of sharing what I had seen of this spiritual attack on the city, but was warned by God that when I shared this it would result in great wrath coming against the city.

My first response to this was not to share anything about it, but I was told that I was to share this and to expect the wrath to come. Later, I was shown that whenever Satan is cast out of heaven, or his realm over a place, that he comes down to the earth with great wrath, knowing that his time has been shortened, just as we see in Revelation 12:12.

How was my sharing the revelation of what the principality was going to do cast him down? It wasn't, but it would begin the process. Satan dwells in darkness, and whenever he is exposed by the light of revelation, it begins to displace him, the same as when a light is turned on in a room, darkness has to flee from it. My sharing this with those who had spiritual authority could have been the beginning of bringing down this form of charismatic witchcraft over the Charlotte region. However, it would not be over with the sharing of the revelation—the battle only began because the devil came down with great wrath.

As I had come to understand the strategy of witchcraft and how it works, I was shown that it attacks like hornets, stinging their victims over and over and driving them out. I was shown what the specific stings were, all of which I have shared in my teachings on witchcraft and counterfeit authority. As this was all fresh to me, it really got my attention when Charlotte's NBA team was named the Charlotte Hornets (they have since moved to New Orleans which is interesting). Did the devil really have a part in naming an NBA team? Why would he do this? First, there is a basic aspect or nature of evil that wants to boast and flaunt itself. This is not to imply that every sports team reflects the evil principality over a region. However, the evil spirit dominating a region will almost always find some way to flaunt itself. Pride and boasting is a basic characteristic of evil, and it simply cannot help itself.

Shortly after my meeting with the church leaders, a storm came off the coast of Africa and was named Hugo, the same name of the Charlotte Hornets' mascot. I'm sure no one in the National Weather Service was making this connection as hurricane names are chosen according to the number of storms that season. However, prophetic people can see connections where others might not see them, and when this storm turned straight for the Carolinas, it got my attention. Even so, it still seemed too far-fetched for this to be what Bob had seen.

The day that Hugo was expected to hit the coast of the Carolinas, I was given a word from the Lord that He would protect me and my family and all that we had. My response was, "From what?" No hurricane had ever come that far inland, and they were just expecting the Charlotte area to get gusts up to 35 mph and a lot of rain. To everyone's astonishment, Charlotte was hit that night with a powerful hurricane. As I looked out of my window that night at the rain coming horizontally, which was maybe ten feet from where Bob had prophesied the "great wind coming against you" and "rain coming horizontally," I knew I was watching a prophecy being fulfilled. I also knew this was the "great wrath" that the Lord had warned me about when I exposed the principality over Charlotte.

Charlotte was devastated. Power was knocked out in some parts for a month. When I looked outside the next morning, the forest that Bob had seen flattened was indeed flattened. I had a little twelve by twelve foot shack that we joked about being "the international headquarters of MorningStar Ministries," and I just knew that all I had in it must have been demolished. To my astonishment, it was not even damaged, though trees were down all around it, some probably coming within inches of it when they fell. We surveyed the rest of the property, and the only damage we could find was a couple of shingles blown off of one of the buildings. None of our neighbors were so fortunate, and we knew we had been protected.

One of the local news stations had surveyed the path of the storm and remarked, "Hugo made a *beeline* for Charlotte." Of course, many made the connection between Hurricane Hugo and the Charlotte Hornet's mascot. Could a little spiritual event such as sharing the nature of a principality stir up such a devastating storm? Yes. This was just the beginning of a long saga that we have had with storms and a long battle we have fought against witchcraft. This thread is woven throughout our history, including storms on the East Coast, Gulf Coast, and the North Sea. The understanding we have gained from all of these storms is considerable, and the stories need to be told.

Though our battle with this charismatic witchcraft is not over in Charlotte, there have been victories and ground has been taken. The result of this is going to be a new breed of leadership arising that walks in true spiritual authority, abiding in the Holy Spirit, and doing His will.

I will have much more to write about storms and witchcraft, but it was no accident that the last place that hurricane force winds were measured from Hurricane Hugo was on the Brushy Mountains in a little place called Moravian Falls. The day Hurricane Hugo hit was also the day that Steve and Angie Thompson joined the staff of MorningStar. We joke that we still don't know who did more damage, but Steve and Angie truly laid a major part of the foundation of what MorningStar has become. The plot will thicken more, and I will get into some things that still astonish me, but they are our history. There is revelation in it that will be crucial for our times.

These were all foretastes of some of the things I had seen in *A Vision of the Harvest*. They were unfolding so quickly that I resolved to write the full vision or it would soon no longer be a vision but a history book. However, I was so busy doing other things that I did not have much time for writing. When I received a word from the Lord that I needed to write the book, I resolved to do it, but was often distracted by all that was happening. This would lead to one of the biggest rebukes and greatest experiences I have ever had.

CHAPTER THREE
FRIENDS OF GOD

After moving to The Lamb's Chapel, I began to meet people who I knew would have an association with me for the rest of my life. Right after Mike Bickle, Bob and Viola Jones, and Jack Deere had first visited us, I felt compelled to visit Jack in Fort Worth to get to know him better.

Jack had become notorious in the Dallas/Fort Worth area because of a feature article about him that had been carried in the Sunday newspaper. This article, titled "True Believer," told of how he had started believing in the present operation of the gifts of the Holy Spirit, which resulted in him being fired as a professor at Dallas Theological Seminary. When Jack started to believe in the present operation of the gifts of the Spirit, he also began moving in them.

Jack put together a small "power team" of individuals who were young in the things of the Spirit but were full of faith to see God heal and cast out demons. They went around ministering to the sick and demonically-afflicted with remarkable results. The reporters from the Dallas paper followed Jack's team for several weeks and were convinced of the truth of the miracles they witnessed. The article was one of the most positive I had ever seen in a secular newspaper written about present-day works of the Holy Spirit.

I was anxious to meet this team and see them in action. However, that was not the Lord's main agenda for us that week. Leesa, Jack's wife, was having powerful prophetic dreams. Because these things were relatively new to them, there was both an excitement about the gifts of the Spirit, as well as faith in them that I had rarely seen in Pentecostal or Charismatic circles. Not only were they new, fresh, and exciting, but they were also free of most of the traditions that had gradually seeped into many Pentecostal and Charismatic movements, which had at times begun to choke out the faith required for operating in the gifts. I felt that this was like a whole new well of living water springing up that was still pure.

By this I do not mean to neglect all that the Pentecostal and Charismatic movements had accomplished, which have been the most effective moves of God since the early church in scope and overall advancement of the gospel. However, decades of attacks and criticisms seem to have stymied many Pentecostal and Charismatic churches from actually operating in the gifts, though they still held to the beliefs that they were for the church today.

There were also movements such as the Full Gospel Businessmen's Fellowship International that the Lord was mightily moving through and where the gifts of the Spirit seemed to operate more freely than in churches. Without question, the Pentecostal and Charismatic movements took more ground and spread the gospel more widely than any previous movements in church history. However, there was something fresh from what I saw breaking out with Jack and his team that I thought could actually result in a fresh move of the Spirit. Later, when I met John Wimber and got to know the Vineyard Movement, I saw the same freshness, so the Spirit was already moving far more than I was aware of at the time.

I also saw in Jack Deere something I had not seen before, which was a profoundly critical attitude about every miracle, checking it out thoroughly to prove that it was real, but with an attitude that wanted to believe, not doubt. Though Jack was still feeling that much of his theological training had only kept him from the present moves of God, I could see then it was also a foundation that would serve him well and could help bring a new level of integrity to the miracle and healing ministries.

Jack was also a Hebrew and Greek scholar, and his theological training caused him to critically evaluate every teaching he heard. Though he was reticent to share little nuances where the Scriptures were not being interpreted correctly, when asked, he could usually bring an insight that brought much greater clarity and accuracy. I could see these things in Jack's principles that could help bring needed challenges to those who moved in the gifts of the Spirit without shutting them down, but in fact free them.

John Wimber

It was also while I was at Jack Deere's house that I had my first introduction to John Wimber. He called Jack one day, and during their conversation, he asked Jack to see if I had a word for him. When I inquired of the Lord for John, He told me to warn him that a scandal was about to be released in The Vineyard. Jack had probably told me some things about John, but I was in something of a spiritual seclusion for seven years while I had been in business and did not know John or many of the other leading figures who had emerged in the body of Christ during that time. Regardless, I did not think this was a very encouraging way to start a relationship with someone, but it was all that the Lord gave me for John.

Of course, John did not want to hear a word like that. However, just a few days later, serious sexual misconduct in one of the leading pastors was exposed, which was the biggest scandal to have hit The Vineyard up until that time. When I heard about the integrity with which John dealt with this scandal, I gained a lot of respect for him and The Vineyard, and I would spend a lot of time with him over the next couple of years.

Though I never became an official part of The Vineyard, it was a very exciting and instructive time for me there. However, I don't remember the Lord ever giving me anything prophetic to share with John that was very positive, but to his great credit, he listened to me and often responded to what I shared with him. I was told that I was one of the few people that he had ever asked to stay at his home for any length of time. He also asked me to speak at his conferences and at his home church in Anaheim, though he did introduce me as "the prophet who never had anything good to say to him."

John was also recruiting Jack Deere to join his staff as the associate pastor at the Anaheim Vineyard Church. John wanted Jack on his team because of the qualities Jack had that I previously described. John wanted to bring much higher standards of accountability to The Vineyard, for not only verifying miracles and healings, but also doctrinally, and he had great respect for Jack. John really cared about these things, but felt that he personally lacked the kind of theological training that was needed to bring correction in these areas. He saw Jack as being especially equipped to help him do this.

It was through John Wimber's leadership that many movements and denominations were inspired to new spiritual heights, as well as greater integrity and accountability. This resulted in untold numbers of people coming to the Lord, and/or being healed and delivered. Even a cursory study of the church through these times would reveal The Vineyard movement as possibly having the greatest impact around the world during the 1980s. In a significant way, John Wimber and The Vineyard movement have also played a major part in preparing the way for the Lord. More will be said about this later.

Certainly other great movements emerged during this time, such as Calvary Chapel, of which The Vineyard movement had been born. The Calvary Chapel movement may not have made many of the spiritual headlines during this period. However, it had accomplished even more during the 1970s and had laid a foundation for longevity and growth that has enabled it to keep on taking significant spiritual ground to this day. However, during the time I am writing about here, The Vineyard was creating huge bow waves as it plunged ahead through the choppy spiritual seas of the times.

It was also through John Wimber and The Vineyard movement that I saw much being done to prepare the way for the coming harvest that I had seen in my vision. Around John and The Vineyard, we witnessed many extraordinary miracles. Also, many important issues were worked out in private gatherings that I feel helped to set the course of my life and shape the direction of much of our ministry. I consider it a great privilege to have been able to spend the amount of time with John that I did, and I consider him to be one of the great leaders of the last half of the twentieth century. I also think that it was through John that many of the great future leaders of the church were called and prepared.

At the time I visited Jack, he was seriously considering going to work for John in Anaheim, but he did not tell me this because he did not want to give any details to prophetic people who might hear from the Lord in a way that would help with such decisions. However, the direction for this move did not come through me, but rather Lessa Deere, who had a dream while I was staying with them that made the direction clear. All I did was help them interpret it. Little did I know that it was about to change my life almost as much as it did theirs.

PAUL CAIN

While I was staying at the Deere's that week, Jack was interested in having me meet a friend of his that he would not tell me anything about. The friend was Paul Cain. The day we were supposed to meet Paul, Jack received an urgent call that Paul was in the hospital with heart problems. We immediately started to pray for Paul, and I had a vision in which I saw Paul in a hospital room. I then saw a spirit of death come for Paul, but it could not touch him. I related this to Jack, saying that Paul was going to be okay.

Later, I received a phone call from Bob Jones, and he asked me what had happened to Paul Cain. I was surprised that Bob even knew Paul, but he went on to relate how he had seen a spirit of death come for Paul, but because it could not touch him, it "jumped on some lady." Though I had not seen the incident with the lady, I was now even more curious about this spirit of death that we had both seen and about who Paul Cain was. I assumed that Bob had also talked with Jack about this vision of Paul and the spirit of death, but I found out later that he had not.

Even so, I was quite surprised when a few hours after we had prayed for Paul that he called Jack and said that he had left the hospital and was at home. He said he had been talking to a woman who was in the cardiac care ward with him who just dropped dead. The doctors had not been able to revive her even though she had only come in for tests and did not have anything seriously wrong with her. This had so troubled Paul that he put his clothes on and left the hospital. This woman was obviously the one who the spirit of death had jumped on when it was thwarted in taking Paul.

This whole series of events stunned me. Little did I know that both the knowledge that I was gaining on the spirit of death, and Paul Cain, would have such an impact on my life and ministry in a very short time. Later, all of these events and people would start to fit together in a remarkable revelation of what I believe will be increasingly important for the last-day ministry of the church. I will share this account later.

The next day Paul came over to Jack's house. As soon as he entered the room, I had a vision of him in a landing craft commanding the waves that were going before him, saying, "I will return." In this vision, I also saw a huge battle taking place on the shore that Paul was headed toward, but he kept going toward it any way. I knew that like General MacArthur, Paul had left something that he had to return to. At the time, I had no knowledge of Paul's previous ministry as a healing evangelist during the great Healing Revival of the 1940s and 1950s, or of his years of obscurity, which he was just about to come out of.

Paul, Jack, and I spent the afternoon together and then went out to dinner. I liked Paul a lot from the very beginning. He had an almost supernatural sense of humor, but from that first day, I was concerned that he seemed far more focused on the past than the present or future. Even so, as he told me about his mother, I knew that there was something important about her and his past that concerned our future.

I was also interested in Paul because at the time he had spent nearly thirty years in relative spiritual obscurity, and I had just come out of seven years of the same. I felt that the waves I had seen in the vision about Paul represented spiritual movements. It was obvious that he would do this during a time of great spiritual battles. In some ways, this all seemed to fit with what I had seen in *A Vision of the Harvest*. At the time, I had only written the brief summary, which had been widely-circulated, but was only a part of what I had been shown. The rest I would later publish in the book, *The Harvest*. I knew there was obviously far more to Paul than I could see at the time, but just being with him and Jack was helping to reawaken some prophetic gifts in me that had been dormant for a long time. Little did I know just how much more there was to him and how he was going to impact our lives for the next few years. I will cover this in some depth later.

THE DINNER

While visiting Jack and Leesa, they planned a dinner party for some friends, but as had already become Jack's pattern, he would not tell me anything about them because he wanted to see what I would receive prophetically. After having come out of spiritual isolation for seven years, I was dull in my prophetic gifts, even though I was making up for lost time quickly. My gift had always been more for seeing major strategic patterns, rather than seeing things for individuals, but at Jack's prodding, I was starting to see things for individuals, too. Even so, I knew whoever was coming to dinner was important because of the way they were preparing for it. This was my first meeting with Kay and Karen Fortson.

Karen was a beautiful girl who was, as I was later told, named one of the most eligible bachelorettes. However, she was on fire for God, having been baptized in the Holy Spirit, and had become a part of Jack's "power team" and was praying for the sick and casting out demons. Kay was also a very beautiful, gracious lady from one of the great oil families in Texas. She and her husband, Ben, had built the Kimbell Art Museum in Fort Worth, housing one of the great art collections in the world. The building they had constructed to house their art had itself been named one of the most important architectural works of the twentieth century. This was typical of the kind of devotion to excellence that was a hallmark of the Fortson family.

Kay, like Karen, was also becoming interested in the deeper things of God. Kay also had a deep concern for her family to live godly and serve the Lord. It was an interesting dinner, and I liked Kay and Karen a lot. As the owner of a large air charter service, I had met many wealthy and powerful people, but I had never met any who had the grace and dignity that the Fortsons had.

They were like true nobility, which was not about wealth but character. Later, when I met Ben Fortson, I knew I had met someone with rock-solid integrity, one who was the "salt of the earth" on a very high level and who could affect business and industry. I also felt from the first time I met them that this family was important to God for this reason. They were called to be a type of standard bearer for integrity in business and culture.

The week at the Deere's was more than a little interesting. I left with many things to ponder and knew that some would dictate our course for years. My visions and new relationships were starting to fit together. It seemed as if I was in some kind of zone where I was constantly meeting some of the most extraordinary Christians that I had ever met. I felt that many would be close friends and co-laborers for life.

FRANCIS FRANGIPANE

Soon after I returned home from Jack Deere's, I got a call from Bob Jones, who told me that I needed to go to Cedar Rapids and meet a man who had a true apostolic calling. When Bob told me his name, Francis Frangipane, my first thought was that if a man had survived a name like that I wanted to meet him! Shortly after that, I got a call from Francis, asking me to come speak at his church. I accepted.

I knew as soon as I met Francis that he was a true pastor. Right after he picked me up at the airport, he took me on a tour of his facilities while trying to discreetly test my doctrine and find out what I was going to share with his church. Even so, I liked Francis, and his wife, Denise, a lot, and they were very easy to be with. We not only seemed to share much in the vision we had for what was coming, but I could tell that Francis had a powerful teaching gift, as well as the gift of a word of wisdom, which I found to be rare in the church.

With the prophetic ministry and gifts that were arising with such power, I had come to believe that the gift of a word of wisdom was the most desperately needed gift in the church, and Francis had it. We would be linked together in many things in the years to come, and we remain close to this day. His steadfast and unyielding desire to know the Lord and be changed into His image has made him a pillar in the church in our times. Like Jack was with doctrine and the testimony of miracles, Ben and Kay Fortson were with business and culture, Francis had a deep devotion to integrity in church life and relationships, which was also a purifying filter for his understanding of spiritual strongholds and spiritual warfare.

Francis and Denise were like undiscovered treasures, with world-class teaching gifts and depths of revelation, but faithfully serving a congregation of just over one hundred people in the city of Cedar Rapids, Iowa. However, like the true shepherds they are, they were serious about their charge, and every man, woman, and child in it. Francis' teaching gift quickly thrust him into international visibility and influence, but to this day, I have not seen his love and concern wane for the River of Life congregation and the rest of the body of Christ in Cedar Rapids. He counseled his local church members with the same care as he would international church leaders. Francis is one of the greatest local church men I have ever met, which is a grace that is critical for our times.

I helped Francis get his first book, *The Three Battlegrounds*, published which instantly became a classic. I consider it to still be one of the best books ever written on spiritual warfare. Not to detract from the importance of that book, but his next two, *Holiness, Truth, and the Presence of God,* and *The Stronghold of God,* are considered by almost all who read them to be even better and probably more important for our times. Those three books alone would almost certainly place Francis as one of the great Christian writers of our times, or of all-time, but they were just the beginning. I also expect these three books to become rediscovered soon, because they are even more relevant now than when they were first published.

Francis and Denise have an interesting and lovable family and a vibrant and solid church life. I was thankful to Bob for encouraging me to get to know them. I was even more encouraged by what I had found with them and in Cedar Rapids at the River of Life Fellowship. Within a year, both became well-known, and people came from around the world to see them.

CHAPTER FOUR
A NEW BREED OF MINISTRY

We moved to Charlotte just after the fall of Jim Bakker, and at that time, a steady stream of people were seeking to take over the PTL ministry property. I had only seen a few PTL programs and thought they were interesting, but personally, I was not comfortable with the style being projected. This is not to imply that I did not think it was good, but it was not my style personally, so I did not give it much thought. However, it was hard to be in Charlotte without listening to the constant talk about PTL, which I would say was still mostly positive. Even so, personally I just did not have any interest in it, so I kind of endured it as being of local importance. However, to honor the local people, I needed to give it some attention. As it became more of a scandal, I really wanted it to just go away.

As my prophetic reputation grew, more people asked me what I thought was going to happen to the PTL property and ministry. I did not have, nor did I want anything from the Lord about it, so I did not seek Him about it. This was really irresponsible on my part because I should have been seeking the Lord about something that was having such an impact on the worldwide body of Christ, not to mention so many of my own neighbors. I did not even take the time to visit PTL until they put the Christmas lights out.

Then a group of businessmen came to plan how they could acquire the property. They really had a heart for the PTL property and wanted to see it stay in the hands of Christians. I liked them even though I was not too keen on their plans. Even so, when they asked me to pray for them and their plans, I had an open vision that would change my heart toward the PTL property. I saw the doors to the Grand Hotel chained shut and the buildings deteriorating. I then saw the Lord Himself walk up to a large round stone and touch it and it rolled aside, opening the grave for what I knew was a resurrection.

I saw the Lord's face in this vision—and this was very important to Him. From that moment, I resolved that it would be on my heart as well. Even so, there were implications to this vision. For something to be resurrected, it would first have to die. PTL was far from dead because Jerry Falwell was trying to make a go of it. Other ministries were circling like vultures, waiting for him to fail so that they could take it over. (At this writing, we have taken possession of some of the key elements of this property, and we can feel the same thing.)

I shared the vision with the businessmen that I was praying for, and anyone else that inquired of me. I was sure that it would die, that it would be closed and the doors chained shut for a time, long enough for it to deteriorate, but it would be resurrected by the Lord Himself touching it. Although I did not see this in a vision, I was later shown that those whom touched this property before the Lord had resurrected it would be seriously damaged, whether they tried to keep it from dying or tried to resurrect it prematurely.

I also remembered James Robison telling me that the Lord was going to use the PTL property. Although at the time I had trouble relating to what he was saying, I now wanted to hear what he had to say about it. When I called him about this, he also used the term "resurrection." He said that the Lord was going to resurrect it because of all of the "widows' mites" that had been sown into PTL. When I called Bob Jones to see if he had anything about this property, he also said that the Lord was going to "resurrect it because of the widows' mites."

After talking to James and Bob, I was even more confident that I had interpreted this vision correctly— that the PTL ministry would have to die and that its doors would actually be chained shut long enough for the property to deteriorate. Then it would be resurrected by the Lord's own hand. I wrote the following in one of the first *Morning Star Prophetic Bulletins*, which was distributed in October 1988:

> *While praying with a group of men who were considering the purchase of this ministry, I saw the Lord walk up to a large stone and as He touched it, the stone rolled*

away and the grave was opened. Knowing this spoke of a resurrection, and being surprised by it, I called Bob Jones in Kansas City to ask if the Lord had shown him anything about PTL. He immediately said that the Lord had shown him that it would be resurrected. He had been shown the widows' mites that had been put into this ministry and the Lord said that He had watched over them, and it was for them that He was doing this. I then called James Robison in Fort Worth and asked him if the Lord had shown him anything about PTL. He said that He had, and that he believed it would be resurrected because of the widows' mites.

A few nights later the Lord spoke to me and said, "When this ministry is resurrected, it will be an eunuch for the kingdom's sake. It will never again rape His bride, but will be used to prepare her for the coming union with Him in harmony with the new breed of ministry about to be released."

Before there can be a resurrection there must first be a death, and this ministry is not yet dead. The Lord is delaying coming to its aid just as He did with Lazarus. The doors will be closed and the grave sealed for a time before He will move. The stone will not be rolled away until He touches it. At that time, it will be given to the stewards He has prepared for a fraction of the present asking price. The new ministry will not be under financial pressure and it will not be a financial burden on the body of Christ.

As is common with many true prophecies, it looked like there was no way for it to be true when I gave it. I even received a few rebukes for "being so negative," declaring that it would have to die before it could be resurrected. As stated, it looked like Jerry Falwell might be able to make a go of it, and there were a host of other large ministries waiting to take it over if he failed. No one wanted to hear my prophecy about this, and few came to inquire of me about this property. However, I warned anyone who came to me and would listen, to not touch it until they were absolutely sure the Lord had led them to do this. I sincerely had no idea that this was for me and that we would end up being the ones who would help resurrect it.

This was also the first prophecy that I could recall about the "new breed of ministry." This actually captured my attention more than the PTL property. To find and help those who were called to be a part of this would become a driving force in everything we did, especially in the founding of our MorningStar School of Ministry (now MorningStar University, MSU), and our K-12 school (The Comenius School of Creative Leadership, CSCL), which we named after Jon Amos Comenius, who is called "the father of modern education." Comenius was a Moravian bishop who gave birth to modern education because of his vision to see a generation prepared to fulfill "the Great Commission." Because he had become one of my heroes in church history, we developed a vision for education for the same purpose—to prepare a generation to fulfill the Great Commission.

The heartbeat of MorningStar has been the preparing of the next generation, but in the wisdom of God it had to be linked to a ministry of the previous one, one that symbolized to many the failure of modern Christianity. "Those who do not learn from history are doomed to repeat it," is repeated to us every day that we walk the grounds of Heritage. We do not want to forget the good or the bad from the PTL history.

PTL may have ended in disgrace, but it was used in a powerful way to change the basic nature of the worldwide body of Christ that will be increasingly crucial for the days to come. Jim Bakker was not only a pioneer in Christian television, he was possibly the most bold ever to invite any person from any denomination or non-denomination to speak from the PTL platform if he thought they had a message that the church needed to hear. This caused Pentecostals to start listening to Baptists, Baptists to start listening to Pentecostals, Charismatics to listen to Presbyterians, and Catholics to listen to all of the above, until a great interchange was occurring that brought unprecedented growth and blessings to the church.

Soon they were all coming to Heritage USA, meeting and having fellowship together. Never in history had a ministry done this before, at least on this scale. The momentum for interchange in the body of Christ has continued, and those churches and movements which have refused to be related to the rest of the church have become increasingly marginalized. Without question, the "new breed of ministry" will be inclusive and secure enough in their own calling to relate to the other members of the body of Christ like the family that we are.

That anointing for fellowship and interchange across the spectrum of the church seems to be prevalent at the resurrected Heritage International Ministries, our name for the Heritage Grand Hotel and Conference Center after we restored it. This was a powerful and prophetic declaration from PTL, and it has been a basic devotion of MorningStar as well, to help promote the unity of the body of Christ that will be required for what is to come.

No doubt the financial mismanagement and other problems that surfaced at PTL would also be a prophetic picture of what much of the church would go through and need to learn from as well. Coming from a business background, I have had a resolve to run MorningStar on sound business principles with a basic vision of helping others to understand the modern business world environment that the church of the twenty-first century must operate in. For this reason, it seems that from the beginning MorningStar has attracted businessmen and businesswomen, and serving them is also part of our basic vision. This was part of who we were long before we inherited the Heritage Conference Center. Through studying what caused the collapse of that ministry and through many hours of talking to Jim Bakker, we have been encouraged to carry this to much greater depth.

Again, my fascination with the "new breed of ministry" was greater than just my interest in the PTL property. As

I pursued understanding this new breed of ministry, I was shown that when the property was resurrected, it would be a training base. I saw a coming Elijah ministry like that of John the Baptist, whose whole vision and purpose was to prepare the way for the Lord by training disciples who would follow Him, who would always point to Him and be willing to decrease as He increased in their lives. Their hearts for the church, the bride of Christ, would not be for anything that she had, but to help prepare her to be a worthy bride for Christ. This is when I formulated my personal motto, which I also made the motto for MorningStar Ministries:

WE WILL NOT USE THE PEOPLE TO BUILD OUR MINISTRY, BUT WE WILL USE OUR MINISTRY TO BUILD THE PEOPLE.

It would be many years before we would come into possession of the former PTL property, but I just wanted to be a part of helping to prepare the new breed of ministry that I was shown would be raised up. Over the years, I was shown many other aspects of this coming ministry, and I still feel that I have much to understand about them. However, it is the basic vision that drove the forming and building of MorningStar and also attracted me to the people we both associated with and brought on as staff at MorningStar.

As all of this was unfolding, and I talked to many of my new friends about the PTL property and what I was being shown, Bob Jones was the only one who seemed interested. He is now living on the grounds.

The Kansas City Fellowship

Mike Bickle had planted a church in Kansas City named simply, The Kansas City Fellowship (KCF). I don't think a ministry could have been more different than PTL. PTL was known for its extravagance, which came from a feeling that "the King's kids" deserved it. Hardly a ministry has ever been more devoted to simplicity, sacrifice, and anti-materialism as The Kansas City Fellowship.

For a period of time in the late 1980s, the PTL ministry of Jim Bakker was without question the most famous ministry in the world. An estimated six million people a year came through the gates at Heritage. After the shaking began with the revelation of Jim's affair, it quickly became infamous around the world.

After the PTL ministry began to crumble, The Kansas City Fellowship may have become the most famous church in the world. It was not only a large and fast-growing congregation, which had spawned several other congregations in the Kansas City area, but it was a movement that was becoming known throughout the body of Christ, especially for the extraordinary prophetic gifts. From my first visit, I felt that it was one of the most unique and exciting churches or ministries I had ever seen, and it became even more so. It, too, would go through its own shaking and might have even become the most infamous in the world for a time, but in this case it was because of false accusations.

The prophetic ministry of Bob Jones was a primary reason for the growing fame and mystique of KCF as the stories about Bob were being spread around the world.

However, there were other prophetic people there, and the heart and substance of KCF was more in intercession and worship than the prophetic. Mike Bickle was also one of the most dynamic preachers to have emerged in the church in many years, and his messages fueled a great and growing fire of passion for the Lord. Altogether this combined for an atmosphere around KCF that was electric with expectation, and there were groups of pastors and people visiting almost continually. Mike and his leaders had all committed themselves to live simply and modestly and took small salaries from the church. Most lived in something of a Christian community that had formed in an apartment complex made up of old but clean and simple duplexes. They drove cars that I thought would have been rejected by some junk yards, and they even liked to boast about whose car was in the worst shape.

Since this was probably the period of the high water mark of "the prosperity gospel," KCF was a remarkable and striking contrast to the times. This was not done in reaction to the prosperity gospel, but rather a desire to follow biblical, apostolic Christianity in its truest, sacrificial form. Because I had just lost our little fortune, I felt that I qualified for the KCF vow of poverty with our living circumstances at the time. However, I had been told when I was first called by the Lord that I would be called to live differently. It takes faith to live and learn to abound or be abased, as the Apostle Paul explained. My goal has not been to be rich or poor in the things of this world, but to be obedient and thankful for whatever I have.

As stated, Mike and his team were embracing what many called "the poverty gospel" while most of the church at the time was into "the prosperity gospel." Mike and his team wanted to stay free from the love of money and to do everything for the sake of the gospel. I believed their sincerity in this and appreciated their devotion to it, though I did not think it was for every church and neither did they. Even so, this was flying in the face of the mentality that was growing in the church in America, which had become a major stronghold, and persecution for it was inevitable. In the groups of visitors, you could often hear both praise for this simplicity and charges of KCF having "a religious spirit."

Though KCF was not the New Jerusalem, it was a remarkable work, and for a period of time it was probably one of the most remarkable churches I had ever known. They were injecting a fresh vision and passion for the Lord into a church falling into increasing confusion and discouragement because of the scandals of the 1980s. For that period of time, KCF had a purity, a zeal for the Lord, and a presence of the Lord like I had not experienced anywhere else. Mike had one of the purest hearts of devotion to the Lord of anyone I had ever met, and those who gathered to him were remarkable people of faith with devotion to the Lord. Even so, the remarkable prophetic ministries of Bob Jones, John Paul Jackson, and others were getting the headlines, as they were no doubt spectacular.

The Kansas City Conference

When Francis Frangipane and I were asked to speak at a prophetic conference hosted by KCF, I was very glad to do so. The conferences at KCF were even more highly charged because people came to them from around the world, and the place was packed. It was a great experience. I have never considered myself a great speaker, and when Mike asked me to share the vision of the harvest that I had received, I felt that it came across especially dry, but the people were so charged, you could have read the ads from the newspaper and received cheers. Many great things happened at that conference, but the teachings of Francis Frangipane on spiritual warfare were the talk of the conference, along with the interview with Bob Jones.

As powerful as the conference meetings were, the real high level things were happening in the hospitality room where the speakers and staff gathered between meetings. I sat with or close to Bob Jones most of the time because the personal prophetic ministry he was doing there was astonishing. When I started to minister with him, I also stepped into a new level of prophetic insight. People were being radically changed, healed, and delivered, and so was I by just being there. After traveling and speaking in many churches and conferences that were good, this was a new level, and I left Kansas City with the greatest hope I had ever had for the church in our times. That hope would grow, and then a great disappointment would come, but this was just the beginning of two of the most powerful years I had ever experienced up until that time.

As stated, I shared with Francis all that I knew about self-publishing so that he could get his book on spiritual warfare, *The Three Battlegrounds,* out as quickly as possible. It was an instant bestseller, and probably remains one of the best and most impacting books ever written on this subject. Praise for that book was being sung across the body of Christ, but it was also stirring up battles! The chapter on the spirit of Jezebel was the source of most of the conflicts. Soon Francis had to have people answering phones to handle the many calls for counseling about how to deal with this powerful spirit, which was indeed gripping much of the church in America as well as the culture.

After the Kansas City Conference, I met people who said they saw me there or had heard the tapes. Almost everyone was excited, but with a few you could discern a subtle jealousy directed at KCF. This concerned me because most of the divisions in the body of Christ were based more in jealousy than doctrine or practice. As we are told in Scripture, Jesus was crucified because of envy, and it was a constant source of persecution against the apostles as well. Even so, the positive people were outnumbering the critics many times over. The positive ones were very positive, and many were being revived with a great hope in the Lord.

CHAPTER FIVE
THE DREAM

A couple of weeks after I met Bob Jones, I received a call from him. He started telling me that the Lord had called me to "the mountains of North Carolina," and that he had seen the place where I was to go in a dream. Having been told myself to go to the mountains of North Carolina, but seemingly not being able to get past Charlotte, I was more than a little interested in this dream.

Bob went on to say that I was called to a place that was one hundred miles from where I was (The Lamb's Chapel) and forty miles from the Tennessee border. To get to this land, we would have to go almost due north on a major highway (which turned out to be Interstate 77), and then west on another highway (which was U.S. 421). He then described the property itself, saying there was a mountain overseeing the property that had a rock face and a beacon on another mountain close by that could be seen from the property. He said that the gospel would go out to the world from that mountain. He also said the land was measured from oak trees to white rocks, and there was a red roofed building in the middle. I asked Bob if the red roof could be a rusted tin roof, and he said that he thought it could be.

Bob went on to share a number of details about this land, which I will cover later. He also said that I was going to meet a man named Ricky Skaggs, who would tell me about his heart for the mountain people when I met him. This man was called to be a part of our ministry. I told him that I had heard of Ricky Skaggs and thought he was a country music singer. Bob said that he had heard of him too, but did not know if this was the same Ricky Skaggs. When I met Ricky some months later, he immediately started talking to me about his heart for the mountain people. I knew this was our man.

I told Harry Bizzell about the dream Bob had. Harry was excited about this dream, but for me, not him. He and Louise were certain that their destiny was in Charlotte and that they would not leave their present location at The Lamb's Chapel. As Harry was telling me this, I looked at the picture hanging above him that I suddenly felt a prophetic anointing on. It was of a chair I recognized in the Bizzell's backyard, but it had mountains in the background. I asked Harry who had painted the picture. He said that his sister had painted it in their backyard and gave it to them as a gift. I asked him why she put mountains in it, and there was a heavy presence that seemed to engulf us both. I could tell that Harry felt it too, but he was adamant that they were not supposed to leave Charlotte. I disagreed, but knew the Lord would have to persuade them.

Soon after this, the Lord spoke to me and said that Harry and Louise's destiny in the mountains was so crucial that it actually held "life and death consequences" for their family. I felt a terrible burden from the Lord about this but did not feel that I could share it with the Bizzells without it seeming manipulative. Even so, I knew I had to share it with them for their sakes. I was clumsy when I shared this burden with them, but they took it graciously, even though they remained adamant that they were called to Charlotte. I felt that I had done all I could and would not say anything else. However, the burden I felt about this would not go away.

Even though Harry and Louise were sure that this purpose in the mountains did not involve them, they were willing to help Julie and me all that they could. Harry and I got out a map to see if we could find a place about one hundred miles from where we were and forty miles from the Tennessee border. There were about six places that fit the description, so we knew we needed more guidance. It was to come through Tom Hess, who called me a few days later from Jerusalem.

TOM HESS AND THE MORAVIANS

Tom has a ministry called The House of Prayer for All Nations, which is based on the Mount of Olives in Jerusalem. People from about one hundred-sixty nations come there to pray, where intercession has been occurring around the clock for many years. Tom is also known internationally as an author. One of his more popular titles,

Let My People Go, traces all of the Scriptures concerning the return of the Jewish people to their homeland and what is yet to come in biblical prophecy relating to the Jewish people. Tom had been given a few tracts of land scattered about the United States, which was to be used for a specific prophetic purpose. He also was commissioned to find the ones that were to be a part of that purpose and to give the land to them that they were supposed to have. One of these plots of land was in North Carolina, and Tom thought of me.

When I asked Tom where this land was, he said it was in a place called Moravian Falls. When I asked him where that was, he did not know. We both speculated that it may have had something to do with the Moravians. The Moravians were true founders for both modern missions, which was my passion, and the modern intercessory prayer movements, which was Tom's passion. Harry and I looked up Moravian Falls on the map, and it looked like it was just about one hundred miles from us and forty miles from the Tennessee border! Then Tom mentioned that the land was surveyed in a strange way—that it was marked from "white rocks to oak trees." I immediately asked Tom to fax the deed. I knew this was the place Bob had seen in his dream.

The Roundtable

Tom said that he wanted to come see us and this land. When he told me when he could come, I was not surprised that it was the same time Bob Jones was planning to visit us again. Harry and I decided to wait and go see the land when Bob and Tom were with us.

In one of the dreams that Bob had received concerning me, I was drawing a sword out of a stone and convening a "roundtable of the prophets." With Bob and Tom coming at the same time, I thought it would be a good time to host a roundtable meeting. Bob agreed. We prayed about who should be invited and set the meeting for the first day that both Bob and Tom would be there.

It was much later when I understood that the very first mention of the word **"prophet"** in Scripture is in the same verse as the first mention of the word **"pray" (see Genesis 20:7)**. Our first roundtable meeting would be convened because the two most powerful intercessory and prophetic ministries that I knew of were coming to visit at the same time. They were both coming because of a place that was one of the smallest dots on the North Carolina map—Moravian Falls. It would be much later that I was to realize just how important this coming together of the prophetic and intercession would be for what was to come in Moravian Falls.

We convened the first roundtable at The Lamb's Chapel, and the interchange was lively. It was very encouraging the way so many Christian leaders were able to discuss issues of substance and depth with such grace toward one another, even when they had differences. I knew then that this roundtable concept had great merit, and in the years to come would, at times, have an amazing impact on events in the church world.

More will be covered on the roundtables later since some of these were truly historic. One of the significant events at this first roundtable was that a number of those attending decided to go to Moravian Falls to see the land that Tom Hess had offered to us, being quite captivated by Bob's dream. I stayed behind, wanting to be a good host to our guests who were not going, but I also wanted to go alone or with a small group when I first saw the land. However, when I heard about the experiences this group had when first going to see it, I was sorry that I had not gone with them. They all came back charged with the prophetic confirmations that they had on the trip. As we were to understand later, when revelation is on such a high, specific, and spectacular level, it is usually because of the difficulty of the task. This would lead to one of the most exciting, but difficult times of our lives.

It is also noteworthy that when we later checked the odometer from The Lamb's Chapel to this land it showed 99.8 miles. Bob had said that it was one hundred, so we chided him, saying that he had missed this one, but he retorted that if we had properly inflated our tires, it would have come out right. When I rode my motorcycle to the Tennessee border to check the mileage, it was close to being forty miles. Impressive, but to prophetic people, this was not just about mileage. One hundred speaks of maximum fruitfulness and forty speaks of testing.

Buck and Elaine Petty

Not long after this, a couple named Buck and Elaine Petty came to meet me at The Lamb's Chapel. As we sat outside with Harry and Louise, I asked them where they were from, and when they answered "Moravian Falls," we all sat up straighter. Before we could say anything, they began to talk about how badly a work needed to be started there, and we knew that it was the Lord speaking through them.

Though we did not connect it at the time, a part of Bob's original dream about the land had included "a white stag" that ruled over the land. I asked Bob at the time if he meant "a white buck," which is what Carolinians call a male deer. Bob said, "Yes, that's what it was." Later, I realized that this was a prophecy of how Buck Petty was called to have spiritual authority over the land that the Lord was calling us to. He does have a special anointing for knowing where roads should be cut, houses and other facilities should be built, as well as who should live there, and at times, who shouldn't live there.

AN ATTACK

A few weeks later, Bob called back with another word about Moravian Falls. He had been shown that Satan himself had sent a "spirit of anger" to thwart our purposes there. I thought it was interesting and encouraging that this was receiving such high-level attention. However, it seemed odd that a spirit of anger would be used to oppose us, but this was about to be revealed quickly.

After visiting Moravian Falls, Julie and I decided to move there. We found a nice little house and decided to offer the owner what he was asking, thinking that it was fair. The real estate agent assured us that the owner would take the offer and would call us that night with the acceptance. That night she called and seemed almost to be in tears. She said that when she gave the owner our offer, he reacted with such rage that they decided to break their agreement to represent him. This did not make sense at all to the agent, especially since we had offered the owner what he was asking. I immediately thought about the "spirit of anger."

We did not pursue that house any longer but decided to wait for more clear direction from the Lord. I was not too concerned about this, since after Hurricane Hugo, it did not seem that a spirit of anger could do too much damage. However, sometimes big attacks are much easier to deal with than smaller ones, especially if they are sustained. This spirit of anger continued to manifest itself, making almost every step of progress difficult.

I then received a word from the Lord that I could not accept gifts for our ministry that had strings attached. That seemed reasonable, and I saw how this could protect us from problems. However, the Lord seemed so adamant about this that I knew it could have importance on a level that I was not aware of yet. Then I heard from Tom Hess, who had to have a board approval to give us the land in Moravian Falls. Tom thought it would be an easy thing, especially with all of the confirmation from Bob's dream and their trip up to see it. When he presented it to this board, they were very excited, but decided they wanted to offer it to us on the basis of a 99-year lease, at $1 a year.

That seemed like a great deal, but I had just heard from the Lord that we could not take gifts with strings attached, and this was a string.

I shared this with Tom, who always esteemed obeying the Lord, and he said he would resubmit it to the board. He didn't think he would have any problems getting it released from those conditions. When he called me back, I could tell even over the phone that he was distressed. He apologized, saying that when he presented what I said to the board, their reaction was with such anger that he actually almost doubted they were Christians.

I told Tom about Bob's word about the spirit of anger, and that I was fine with not receiving this land from them. It had at least been used to help us locate Moravian Falls, and I had no doubt we could find plenty of land for sale there. However, the matter was not over. Donations to Tom's ministry dried up until he was later counseled by Paul Cain to give the land back to whoever had given it to him. Paul knew nothing of the situation with the Moravian Falls property. However, he told Tom that he had some property with an important destiny on it that was being wrongly tied up, and that he should give it back to those who had given it to him so that this judgment would come upon them and not Tom's ministry. As soon as Tom signed the land back to those who had given it to him, donations started pouring back in to his ministry again.

One of the main purposes I have for sharing this prophetic history is for the lessons it contains. God's ways are higher than our ways. We often consider that His attributes are like ours because we use many of the same terms as human attributes, such as love, anger, or jealousy. When the Lord says that He is a jealous God, we should understand that His jealousy is not like human jealousy. Human jealousy is usually rooted in selfishness, suspicion, and fear. God's jealousy is rooted in love, and even His anger is rooted in love. God's jealousy over the land in Moravian Falls was such that He severely disciplined some people who may have seemed to be innocent, like Tom. It was not a form of retaliation, but a protection of His purposes. The more we mature, the more we need to understand this. The things you can get away with in the Outer Court can get you killed in the Holy Place. This incident with Tom and the land put the fear of the Lord in many of us, and I think at least helped prevent a level of presumption about the destiny of Moravian Falls that would protect us from many mistakes in the future.

The Sacrifice

All of this increased my resolve to move to Moravian Falls, but it also increased my fear of the Lord in some needed ways. The destiny on this land was so important that presumption could carry serious consequences. Then, something else happened that imparted an even greater fear of the Lord in regard to this.

As I mentioned before, I had been compelled to share a warning with Harry and Louise Bizzell—that their calling to move to Moravian Falls was so important that it held "life and death consequences for their family." A few months later, Harry accompanied me to Kansas City where we spent some time with Bob Jones. When praying for Harry and Louise, Bob saw a death in the family coming before the Bizzells moved into their purpose. Harry and I assumed this would be his mother, who was very old and was becoming senile. This was not the case. Not long after this, a young granddaughter of Harry and Louise's died in a tragic car accident.

Spicer had been our babysitter, and Anna and Aaryn, our daughters, loved her. When we got the news of her death, Anna, who was six at the time, began wailing with a mourning deeper than I had ever heard from an adult or child. She could not be consoled, and it went on for hours. It was such an obvious spirit of intercession that you could not help but to pray yourself as she wailed. As I was praying for the Bizzells and Spicer's parents, the Wallaces, I was shown that Spicer had been a great lover of God and had prayed and offered herself for the purposes of God, even to the sacrificing of her own life if it served His purpose. She had done this with sincerity, and in heaven she is a martyr who laid down her life for the purposes of the Lord. Spicer Wallace did not die in vain, and she has a great investment in her family's destiny and in the Moravian Falls project. Soon after her death, the Bizzells bought land in Moravian Falls, and they moved there, preceding me by several years.

A New Beginning

Harry and Louise Bizzell have been two of my favorite people since I first met them in the mid 1970s. The more I got to know them and their family, the more I considered them spiritual royalty. They have endured many tragedies and hard and confusing times, but I have never heard anything but faith and trust in the Lord come from them. This does not mean that they have been perfect. It is likely that no one ever passes one of God's tests with a perfect score, but compared to anyone else I have known closely, they have been rock solid in their faith, and faith pleases the Lord. The Bizzells have also helped countless other people along in their sojourn. They made their own sojourn to Moravian Falls and planted a standard there. When anything significant emerges there, they must be considered true spiritual fathers and mothers of it, along with Buck and Elaine Petty.

Harry and Louise also helped lay a foundation for MorningStar Ministries, though they have never been an official part of MorningStar, and we have never been an official part of The Lamb's Chapel. Neither of us ever felt that an official relationship was necessary, but consider true spiritual unity to be better displayed by different and unique ministries that are all being able to love each other and work together without being forced to join each other or be under the compulsion of an official organization. Now there are a number of different ministries on the mountain which enjoy fellowship with one another but are also free to pursue their own visions and purposes. True unity is a unity of diversity, not conformity. It is not likely that the ultimate unity of the body of Christ that is coming will be an official unity but rather a unity of the Spirit that transcends any official relationship.

Before moving to Moravian Falls, Harry and Louise built a lodge in the middle of an apple orchard. Local lore says that the apple orchards that grace the Brushy Mountains were first planted by Johnny Appleseed. Most history books leave out one of the most important aspects of Johnny Appleseed's life—that he was an evangelist and he used apple seeds to preach the gospel. One of his famous sayings was, "You can count the seeds in an apple, but you cannot count the apples in a seed." He went about planting seeds that have now produced countless millions of apples throughout this region. As the Lord declared in Genesis, seeds would only produce after their own kind (see Genesis 1:11). Apple seeds will forever produce apples, not oranges, grapefruit, or anything else, only apples. Therefore, beginnings are important. What was the spiritual seed that the Moravians planted there? What kind of seeds are we planting?

As I came to visit Harry and Louise occasionally, I yearned to join them and move to that mountain. However, I had also fallen in love with Charlotte, and the seeds we had planted there were growing as well. Then I remembered one of the original words that the Lord had given to me about moving to North Carolina, which was in Deuteronomy 28:3, **"Blessed shall you be in the city, and blessed shall you be in the country."** I knew then that our home was to be in both places. I began earnestly praying for a place in Moravian Falls. When a section of forty-six acres became available that ran along the ridge above the Bizzell's, I bought it. After this a little cabin became available on the same road just below The Lamb's Chapel property, and I bought that as well.

CHAPTER SIX
A VISITATION

One day Bob Jones called me with the most stunning revelation that he had received for me yet. He said that I was going to receive a personal visitation from the Lord and a commission directly from Him. This was sobering enough, but he went on to tell me when it would happen. I was a little afraid but also excited. I was also busy, too busy, and being too busy almost cost me my real calling and destiny, as well as this visitation.

As stated, because of the circulation of the pamphlet I had written titled, *A Vision of the Harvest,* and the way my first book, *There Were Two Trees in the Garden,* had been so well received, I was receiving many requests for ministry. Much of my attempt to take ministry invitations was fueled by how I had been called back into ministry after the collapse of my business, and I had a young family to take care of. I'm not saying this was right, but it was true. Even so, there was something else that drove me even more.

I had received a warning from two different people, from different parts of the county, who I knew did not

know each other. They both came to me in the same week
with the same word—that if I did not go as the Lord sent
me, He would give my commission to someone else. As a
result, I was going as fast and often as I could and was on
the road almost constantly, not wanting to lose my commission, even though I was not sure what it was. However,
I was overshooting the runway! This is when I learned that
there is a ditch on either side of the path of life, and if
you overreact to one, you are in danger of falling into the
one on the other side.

The date Bob had given me for the visitation passed
with no visitation. Because the Lord had also spoken to me
about a new commission that I was to receive, I knew it
was supposed to happen, but just figured Bob had the date
wrong. However, as I would soon find out, Bob had been
right, but I was so out of position that the Lord had not
been able to come! This was to lead to one of the greatest
lessons of my life.

James Robison asked me to come back and do a few
television shows with him, and since James had been the
one that the Lord used to put my ministry on the map, I
resolved to always give him top priority when he asked me
to do something with him. I also loved being with James
because of his devotion for seeking the things that were
on God's heart, which was infectious.

After we had taped a few shows, James and I were
sitting in his office when he started to firmly rebuke me
for being too busy and taking too many meetings. The
anointing on him was so strong that I knew this was from

the Lord, and after leaving his office, I went to where I could pray earnestly about what I should do. The Lord spoke to me immediately and told me to cancel the rest of the meetings that I had scheduled on that trip and go home. Julie and the girls were on their way to Louisiana to meet me on this trip, where Bob Jones and I were to minister together. I was surprised when Julie and Bob accepted my cancellation so easily, and I immediately got in the car and drove straight home, praying the whole way.

The Lord had spoken to me before the time with James and said that I was five months behind in the main thing that He had given me to do that year because I had over-extended myself. This really got my attention while I was on the road and had time to think about it. I realized that it had been five months to the day from when Bob had told me I was going to have a visitation from the Lord and the new commission.

I came back to an empty house and began reading a Scripture that the Lord had given me on the way home, which was in Genesis 26. When I came to verses 23-24, **"Then he went up from there to Beersheba. The LORD appeared to him the same night,"** the Lord spoke and said to prepare myself because He was coming to me that night. I did not know what I needed to do to prepare for this, but He spoke again and simply told me to go to bed. I thought there would be no way I could fall asleep, knowing that the Lord was coming, but after turning off all the lights, I did.

The Lord must have put me to sleep because the next thing I remember is waking up feeling a presence in the house. The house was also full of light, and I distinctly remembered turning all of the lights off. My first thought was that my neighbors must have thought that I was still away and were using the house for something, which was not uncommon at the Christian retreat center where we were living. Before I could get out of bed to see what was going on, the Lord walked into my room. He was the Light that was in the house.

Stunned, I buried my face in the pillow and could not get the courage to look at Him. He came over and I felt His hands grip my shoulders. When He did this, something like an electrical current started building up in me. Just when I did not think I could take another second of this without exploding, He lifted His hands and the power receded. He did this over and over for a few minutes and then He started to walk out. I turned over to see Him when He turned back and said, "Bob Jones will explain this to you." The next thing I remember is waking up in the morning.

When I woke up, I instantly remembered what had happened. I lay in bed for a few minutes, wondering if the visitation had been real or if it had just been a dream. If it was a dream, it was more real than any dream I had ever had. I reached for my clothes that were draped over the end of the brass bed and immediately a surge of the power I had felt when the Lord laid hands on me built up, and electricity arched from my hand to the bedpost. I carefully got up and dressed, being afraid to touch anything metal because the surges of power kept going through me in waves. They were not as strong as the night before, but they were still strong, almost to the point of taking my breath away. I knew for sure that whether it was in a dream or had been real, I had been touched by the Lord. I was also bothered that I could not remember how many times the Lord had laid hands on me because I knew this was important.

I went next door to see Harry and Louise Bizzell, and before I could say a word, Harry said, "You had a visitation from the Lord!" He could see and feel it on me, and I think my hair started turning gray that night. I told them all about it, and Harry recommended that I call Bob Jones to get the explanation just as the Lord had said.

When I got Bob on the phone, I started apologizing for abandoning him to do the meetings by himself in Louisiana, but he was okay with it. I had resolved not to tell Bob about the visitation so he would get it straight from the Lord, but he did not seem to know anything about it. However, he said that while praying the night before, he had never seen the heavens so stirred up like that unless Jesus Himself passed through them. He felt that someone had received a visitation from the Lord. I said nothing.

The next day Bob called back saying he had received an angelic visitation and the angel had told him about my visitation. Bob described it just as it had happened, making a special point to tell me how many times the Lord laid hands on me and why. It had not been a dream. The Lord had actually come and laid hands on me. I was both thrilled and sobered. I had received the commission, but it would still take faith and patience to fulfill it.

When I called Jack Deere to tell him about the visitation, he said he wanted to be with me when I laid hands on the sick because he felt this must be a release of great power. I could not wait to do this, but even more so, I expected the prophetic gift that I had been given would go to a new level. After a few weeks, I still could not tell whether any of this had happened, and if anything, I felt less power and less prophetic. This, too, was the Lord, because it is likely that I would have started immediately traveling again to use these greater gifts and would not have finished what He had given me to do. I was already five months behind in writing the full vision of the harvest that I had received the year before, so I got right to work on it. When I finished it, I titled it, *The Harvest.* It quickly surpassed *Two Trees* in distribution and ignited an even bigger wave of interest in our ministry.

CHAPTER SEVEN
A NEW BEGINNING

In 1988, Bob Jones gave me another remarkable prophecy. He said a new birth was coming to Julie and I that would be a sign of a new beginning and a new kind of ministry that was coming to the church. To confirm this word, the new one would come on August 8 and weigh exactly 8 pounds. Julie and I were not expecting to have any more children, so I wondered how this was going to be fulfilled. Two years later, on August 8, 1990, at 8:00 a.m., Amber Grace Joyner was born to us, and she weighed exactly 8 pounds.

At the time, Bob was also in the middle of working on another prophecy that he talked about quite a bit. The Lord had told him that he had "lost his marbles in the garden," a parable of how mankind went crazy when they disobeyed Him in the Garden of Eden. Bob later found some marbles in his literal garden, and in them there was a message about what it would take to restore our spiritual sanity.

While cultivating his garden, Bob had started to find marbles, each a different color and having a different story.

Bob ultimately found twelve marbles in his garden, which he kept. On the day Amber Grace was born, August 8, or 8/8, he found an 8th marble in his garden, and it was amber-colored, which speaks of the glory of God. When I called Bob to tell him about Amber's birth and how the prophecy had been completely accurate, he told me about this amber marble, and I knew right away that Amber was to be her name.

Amber's older sisters, Anna and Aaryn, have both displayed remarkable prophetic gifts. They have also gone through years of not experiencing much, and at times have gone through the usual trials and problems that most of us go through as we seek to find our way. The Lord spoke to us about each of our children before they were born, telling us of their callings and their natures, which we have watched unfold and mature in each one. However, Amber is a prophecy of a new kind of ministry and a new beginning for the church. I have watched her life with special interest to see the signs of this, but this is another story, which I will write about at the proper time.

When I finished the book, *The Harvest,* it kicked off even more interest in *Two Trees* so that it had another big surge. I began to see a distinction in the pattern of those who invited me to minister because they had read *The Harvest* or those who had been touched by *Two Trees.* Those who asked me to come because of *The Harvest* were noticeably livelier and more zealous for the Lord, and those who invited me because of *Two Trees* were noticeably deeper into the Scriptures and sound teaching, but were often a bit dry. I often wanted to get these two groups together because I could see how much they needed each other. This gave me an even greater understanding of why the prophets and teachers needed to learn to serve the Lord together before He could release true apostolic ministry in the earth again. It also fueled my understanding of how the whole body of Christ needed each other. "Cross pollination" and interchange between the movements and denominations in the church became a basic devotion of mine.

The Cabin

As mentioned, Steve and Angie Thompson had come to work for us, along with Roger Hedgspeth. Without them, we would have never been able to keep up with the orders and shipping of our books. It was obvious that we had outgrown our little cottage and one room office at The Lamb's Chapel, so I started looking for a warehouse and offices. Harry said he knew of some property nearby that was unoccupied that might be perfect for our ministry. He called it "the Yager property" because it belonged to Dexter and Birdie Yager, who had one of the largest organizations in Amway, as well as owning a number of other businesses in Charlotte.

When we drove to look at the Yager property, it was far bigger and better than I could have ever dreamed of actually acquiring. It had a log cabin that was over 12,000 square feet, which I was told was one of the nicest ever built, and was the second largest residential log cabin of its type. There was another home on a small lake, a warehouse with offices, and an executive office building with offices so nice that I thought it might make the Oval Office look shoddy. Even though our ministry was growing fast, I still did not think that there was a way we could afford any of it, much less all of it, but Harry prodded me to have some faith and pursue it. I got Dexter's phone number and called him.

Dexter seemed interested in leasing this property, but when he asked me how much I could afford, and I told him $2,000 a month, he laughed and said that would not even be enough to fix the floors if I scratched them. I figured I was offering him less than 5 percent of the retail rental value, and I was just hoping not to offend him. After he asked if I was serious, and I told him that I was, he surprisingly said that he would pray about it. A few days later, he called and said that he would love to see the property used by a ministry. He would lease the log cabin to us for what I offered, and as we grew, we could take over the rest of the property. Dexter was my new best friend!

I have been in a lot of nice homes, but the log cabin was the nicest I had ever been in. It was just perfect, high quality, comfortable, and very spacious. Julie and I had left our dream home and property in Mississippi to move to North Carolina in obedience to the Lord, and in just over a year we were in a place far better than our dream home! It was not ours, but the deal we had with the Yager's made it better than owning, since the property taxes were probably more than we were paying in rent.

As we moved into this property, I learned the history of it. The Yagers love people, and after building it, they only lived in it a few weeks before deciding to move because it was too secluded. It then sat empty for a long time. When Jim Bakker resigned from the PTL ministry, Dexter offered it to him. They moved in and *The Jim & Tammy Show* was taped in the den of the cabin because they were trying to keep their ministry going before Jim was sentenced to prison. After he went to prison, it sat empty until I called.

The cabin was so big that Steve and Angie decided to move into it with us. At times, we had other families living with us too. There was so much room that we never felt like we were getting in each other's way. We had a place for our offices, inventory, and shipping, and we were able to invite many visitors who were coming through. The kitchen/dining room was one big room, large enough for us to eat our meals together, so we bonded as a team very fast. Steve and Angie were doing a great job organizing things, and because I was still traveling so much, it was also great to know that my family had support and help if they needed it while I was away.

The Dream

It took us several months to furnish the cabin, and it made the most peaceful, wonderful home we could have ever dreamed of. Then one night, I dreamed of a large corporation that was having a board meeting in the room behind the fireplace. I knew it was from the Lord, and when

I inquired about what it meant, I was told to be ready to give the cabin up to a large corporation that was coming to ask for it. I sure did not want to hear that, and neither did our staff.

Just a few days later, Dexter called and told us that DuPont Corporation wanted to lease and possibly purchase the property for a corporate retreat and training center. Dexter said that we had a lease, and the only way he would do this was if we agreed to whatever DuPont offered us to buy out our lease. I said I would talk with them, and knew I could not stand in the way of an attractive business deal for someone who had been so generous to us. I also knew that this was what the Lord had said we should do through the dream. We were sad, but this would turn into one of the greatest encouragements that we had received concerning the Lord's special care for us, which helped to lead us into one of our ultimate callings—restoring Heritage USA.

DuPont agreed to buy out our lease, pay us for all of the furniture we had bought to furnish the cabin, let us keep it, and move us at their expense into houses that Dexter was providing for us without charge. Like most young ministries, we were hanging on the edge financially every month, and this instantly gave us the provision to expand our operations. Even so, it was a sad time as we were moving out of the cabin. For some reason, we all gathered and started to dream about what we would do if the cabin was ours—how we would expand the garage, adding French doors, making it into a meeting room, and other such changes that would have made it the perfect place for us. Then we drove off thinking that this very special and happy time had only lasted a few months, but we knew it was the Lord's will for us to go. Without that dream, I don't think we would have given it up.

Just a few months later, the Lord spoke to me and said to prepare to move back into the cabin in October. I had trouble believing this until Steve went to the cabin to see how the DuPont team was doing and noticed that they had done all of the things we had dreamed of doing, only they did it much better! They had put French doors in the garage and even doubled the size of it to make a much larger meeting room. Not long after this, an executive from DuPont called and said that the property was not working out for them and if we would move back they would pay for us to move back. Since they had paid the lease through the next year, we would not have to pay rent until that time was up. They had spent hundreds of thousands of dollars to remodel the cabin, paid for our furniture, gave us thousands of dollars for our lease, and then paid our lease for more than a year, while paying for us to move back. Needless to say, we prayed a blessing for DuPont.

We were back in our dream house, which was now a seemingly perfect base for the ministry. It was even better now than if we had remodeled it ourselves. The Yagers, who watched all of this, knew that the Lord was with us and gave us great favor for just about anything we asked. The lessons we learned in all of this would bear more fruit in the future. There is an interesting link between the cabin and the former PTL property, and the lessons we were learning on the Yager property were preparing us for a much bigger task. Hardly a mile through the woods was Heritage USA, which at the time was beginning to change hands repeatedly.

CHAPTER EIGHT
VICTORIES AND DEFEATS

The year 1988 was one of the most eventful years of my life, and the year in which the foundation of MorningStar was truly laid. Already I could see that it had the potential to be bigger than the aviation company I had shut down the year before. This was a year of the most extraordinary favor of the Lord. But 1989 was to be even more dramatic and wonderful, as well as the beginning of trials.

I understood that there could not have been the kind of impact that the prophetic was beginning to have without persecution arising. I had been waiting for a big backlash, but when it came, it was far more ruthless, cruel, and deceptive than I was expecting. For about two years, it was like living in a modern-day Book of Acts, except with little opposition or troubles. When they came, it was like it had been saved up to hit us from many sides at once in an overwhelming force. Even so, the power and closeness of the Lord had been so great that I could not imagine that the onslaught could even begin to budge us off course. I was wrong.

When there are serious and libelous charges made against you, it is usually necessary to answer them. There are times when the Lord wants us to hold our peace and let Him defend us, as we see a couple of times in Scripture. However, there are many more times when God's people had to defend themselves, as they almost always did in the New Testament. The Lord usually wants to raise up a standard of truth when the enemy comes in like a flood. Truth must be stated boldly to cast out lies, and even some of the New Testament Epistles are the result of this. However, if we start trying to appease the accuser by compromising, we will fall or at least be knocked off course.

Therefore, all persecution should be taken seriously, and we should be careful to get the mind of the Lord about how to respond. We must be careful not to allow it to occupy more of our attention than pressing on to do the Lord's will. However, if you do not answer it, then the lie will prevail. It is my opinion that this is what happened when the persecution arose against the prophetic—leaders counseled the prophetic people not to respond so as not to cause an even further division in the body of Christ. They assured us that they would answer the charges and defend the prophetic, and then they did not do it.

Just about every prophetic person I knew felt betrayed, and some let this turn into resentment and bitterness. Because "a root of bitterness springing up will defile many" (see Hebrews 12:15), soon they were doing things for which they deserved to be persecuted. So in some ways 1989 was the best year yet, and in some ways it was the hardest.

Along with the spectacular words that would amaze and attract people, there were just as many hard words and warnings that we had to deliver, and the consequences of people not hearing them could be a big backlash. At times, I felt that I would only be given hard words for people that I liked the most, and the good, encouraging words for the people I had problems with. Every prophetic person I knew was being tested by the words they were giving to others, and these were not easy tests. I don't think anyone passed these tests with a perfect score.

New Zealand

I had begun to understand how spiritual authority is founded on love, as we see Jesus becoming the Shepherd when He felt compassion for the people who were like sheep without a shepherd. He became their teacher when He felt compassion on the people who lived in darkness. So I began to discern that the Lord was going to send me to a place when I started having a love for it. For many years, I had a fascination and attraction to New Zealand, which I began to understand was one of the ways the Lord calls us to a place. When I got an invitation to go there, I was excited about it, especially when it included Francis Frangipane.

Just a couple of years before this, New Zealand had been called "the most heathen nation on the earth," by a major Christian ministry because it was only a fraction of one percent Christian. However, through the extraordinary ministry of Trevor and Jan Yaxley, and others the Lord was raising up there, it was beginning to experience such revival that it would soon be considered nearly 20 percent Christian. These were real Christians, born again, and on fire for God. There were traffic jams and overflow crowds everywhere we went on that first trip, and I was brimming over with hope for the whole body of Christ when I saw what was happening there. I was also falling even more deeply in love with New Zealand and her people.

When flying into New Zealand, I had seen in a vision one of the native islanders standing with dung covering his head and shoulders. When I shared this in the first church where I spoke, immediately after the meeting they took me down to the harbor to see the statue of a native Maori where the pigeons had covered his head and shoulders in dung, just as I had seen in the vision. I knew this represented the injustice done to the Maoris, and that such injustices could open a gate of hell into a nation, which had been the case in New Zealand. Since then, New Zealand has done much to redress this and make things right with the Maori people. I think this was the result of the church there taking up this issue and proclaiming it.

There is much more to this story, some of which I will share in another volume of this history, but New Zealand has a special part to play in the last-day purposes of the Lord. The city which is literally "the uttermost place on the earth," or the farthest from Jerusalem where this word was given, is Christchurch, New Zealand, which was built by pioneers who had a vision for a city being built that was a city for God. My love for New Zealand and the visions I was given for its future began in 1989. I also felt that the ordeal that Trevor went through was a prophecy of what the nation would go through before it fulfilled its destiny. Trevor overcame his injuries and so would New Zealand.

One of the hardest words I ever had to give anyone was to Trevor Yaxley. When visiting Trevor and Jan's ministry at Snells Beach, New Zealand, Trevor took me to the site where his teenage son had been killed in a car accident. It was also the place where Captain Cook's men had slaughtered the native Maori people when they first landed on the island. I could feel the ground still crying out because of the blood that had been shed there. Death was still strongly in the air, to the degree that I was looking around to see if we were about to be attacked somehow. Then in a vision I saw Trevor having a bad accident in the very same place.

I kept this vision to myself for days, but the burden got heavier. I finally prayed and said that if Trevor came out to see me at the Auckland airport when I had a layover on my way home from Christchurch, I would tell him. As I should have expected, Trevor and his wife Jan called and asked if they could come visit with me during my layover. As we were having coffee, I told them what I had seen in the vision. They took it with wisdom and maturity. I could give them no encouragement that this was a warning so that it could be avoided. Just a few days after I arrived back home, I received the news that Trevor had been in an accident in the place I had warned them about, and that he was seriously injured.

Trevor recovered, but for a long time it seemed that he would be crippled for life. With amazing faith and fortitude, he took this great trial with the encouragement that the Lord works all things for good. I knew that no matter what happened, Trevor and Jan, and many of those who were with them, would stand in victory. I don't think I have found as much courage and fortitude among a people as the New Zealanders, and the Yaxleys represented some of the best.

The End of Communism

It was at about this time that the Lord started to speak to us about being called to help prepare the church in the West for great difficulties that were coming. A few years earlier, Paul Cain had received a word that "communism would become *commu-wasm,*" but that the remnants of communism would combine with Islamic extremists to form a force more dangerous to world peace than communism had ever been. This is now proven history, but at the time it was quite a stretch to believe.

What I had been shown in the vision that I wrote about in *The Harvest* was that the nations that had been under the communist yoke were about to start experiencing increasing freedom, and that the nations that had enjoyed freedom and democracy were about to experience an increasing loss of liberty.

The tearing down of the Berlin Wall and the subsequent collapse of the Iron Curtain were faster and more dramatic than I'm sure any of us foresaw. However, the collapse of communism was the result of a gradual eroding over a long period of time until it all at once fell. The same has been happening in the United States but in reverse. We have had a gradual eroding of our liberty and the foundations of our strength, which has suddenly accelerated. Very few who suffered under the oppression of communism probably suspected that their lives could change so fast, and few in the West probably think the same. It will if we do not wake up fast.

BOB WEINER

At about this same time I met Bob Weiner. It is not a coincidence that I write about him immediately after this word about the end of communism. Bob has been instrumental in helping bring down some of these great strongholds. He was one of the first, and possibly the most effective, at moving into those countries immediately after the Iron Curtain fell to start a large and effective free church movement in communist and former communist nations. Much more will be said about this in a later volume because it is one of the great stories that would certainly be included in any Book of Acts about the last-day ministry.

I met Bob through a couple who I had met that had an increasingly popular children's ministry, but I had discerned something dangerous in it. When I heard that this couple was getting close to Bob's ministry, Maranatha, I was alarmed, but didn't know Bob, so I didn't think that it was any of my business. Then the Lord let me know that it was my business if I was going to be about His business—this was about His family and I would not be a true shepherd if I did not warn His children when I saw danger.

The danger I felt from this couple was for child molesting. I did not know how to share something like this with what would appear to be vague discernment, so I prayed for the Lord to give me some kind of evidence. I was surprised at how fast that prayer was answered. I happened to meet some people who had been in a church with this couple when the problem of child molesting surfaced, which was a major contributing factor in the destruction of that church. I called Bob immediately.

I was relieved by how graciously and wisely Bob received this warning. He saw and appreciated this couple's genuine anointing for children, but had already become concerned about some things and was being cautious. In just the few minutes we talked, I became impressed with Bob's zeal for the Lord and His people. I looked forward to meeting him, which I did soon after at a conference in Kansas City.

Bob was one of the most sincere, bold, pushy, and opinionated people I had ever met, and the only one I had met who was actually anointed to be that way. I really loved all of this about him. His boldness was rooted in a sincere faith, and he was pushy when people needed pushing to get moving. His opinions were also remarkably wise and accurate. I liked him immediately and felt that the Lord showed me that he was going to be a man of true apostolic stature. Every prophetic person I knew saw Bob as a man who would be used to bring millions into the kingdom.

I had been around many over the years who tried to share the Lord with everyone they met, but just weren't anointed to do it. These incidents seemed to be more embarrassing than effective. With Bob Weiner it was different. He had the grace to sow seeds of the gospel with every waiter or waitress, every shopkeeper, even people he casually met on the street, and often got immediate results. His zeal never waned, and it was infectious.

The more I got to know Bob, the more he seemed like a modern Elisha, who was plowing with twelve yoke of oxen when Elijah found him. Like Elisha, Bob did everything that he did big. He saw the nations, and had a strategy he was implementing to reach multitudes, but then unlike so many who have such expansive vision, he would back up and start formulating a practical way to achieve the vision. He always seemed willing to roll up his own sleeves and get started witnessing to individuals.

I have told people for years that Bob Weiner's biggest problem was going to be that there was only one world to save. I have now known Bob quite well for more than twenty years and still consider him one of the most remarkable and effective men of God that I have ever met. His wife, Rose, is filled with the same love for God—radical, enduring fortitude. All of their children seem destined to accomplish great things for the kingdom.

More on John Wimber

I also became much more impressed with John Wimber as I got to know him. My first word for him was not an easy one, but he still wanted to hear from me. In our first real meeting, I had to give him another warning that I delivered in a way that could have been really offensive to him. He received it with genuine openness and grace. I really liked John and felt that Carol was one of the most truly noble women of God that I had ever met. However, I was a bit blinded to their authority and stature in the Spirit, which I did not fully see until after John died.

In spite of me being so obnoxious, John and Carol invited me to come stay in their home for three days, which I was told he had never done before. I was even more impressed with him and Carol as I observed them in their home, but it was hard, awkward, and at times, a very trying three days, probably much more for them than for me. Even so, John continued to invite me to his conferences and church. When I look back on John and Carol's patience with me, I am still amazed by their grace, and pray that I can be the same with others. Now, twenty years later, I continue to glean wisdom from some of the things John and Carol shared with me during those three days.

The more I traveled during those years, the more I realized that John Wimber was one of the most influential men in Christianity at the time. According to Christian leaders I talked with from Europe to the Far East, he probably did more than any other individual to bring respect and credibility to the present operation of the gifts of the Spirit. He was as vocal about his mistakes and flaws as he was with the great miracles that the Lord was doing through him and other Vineyard leaders. He was an honest man, and the Lord trusted him with great spiritual authority.

Like most who carry the kind of responsibility that John did for so many churches and ministries, even a single statement made by him could have a major impact. However, he could be reactionary and short-tempered at times, and this did cause problems. Even so, he loved God, loved people, and he loved the truth. He ruthlessly required that all reports of miracles or other spiritual events be reported accurately. He required failures to be held up just as much as successes. Around the world, John Wimber became like the antithesis to "the ugly American." He did not build his ministry on hype and self-promotion, but on the anointing.

John Wimber was truly a great man of God, and I consider it a great privilege to have known him. I learned much from him and would have learned more if I had not been so proud at the time I knew him. I did have some disagreements with John. I am sure I was wrong about some of these, but I continue to believe that I was right about one. The conflict that I had with John over this issue helped to set the course for my own ministry and MorningStar. It came to the surface when John, Paul Cain, Mike Bickle, Jack Deere, and I were staying together for a few days at a friend's ranch in Texas.

While we were sitting around the fireplace one afternoon, John said that he thought I should start putting footnotes in my books and writing in a style that would be respected by theologians and scholars. I asked him why I should do that since I wasn't writing for theologians and scholars. John replied that if we reached the theologians and scholars, we would reach the rest of the people too. I countered that if that were true, why did the Lord rejoice that the Father had hidden His truth from the wise and intelligent and revealed it to babes?

John was adamant, and so was I. Then Paul came into the room, having just awakened from a nap. He said that he had received a powerful prophetic dream in which he was shown why John the Baptist was angry when the Pharisees and high religious people came to him for baptism. John the Baptist understood how these types could corrupt a movement, how it was his purpose to raise up the valleys and low places, while bringing the spiritual mountains down. I took this as a clear endorsement of my position, but John was not convinced. It was finally acknowledged that John and I had different callings to different people, just as Peter had been called to the Jews and Paul to the Gentiles. This is not to put my calling on the level of John's, but that it was different to different people.

This conflict was not over. John remained adamant that he wanted me to change my style of ministry to make it more appealing to theologians. I thought that it was this devotion of his that was compromising the power of what he was called to do and was sidetracking The Vineyard.

So I left the ranch feeling pressure to change my style of ministry, which I had no intention of doing without a directive from the One that I had received my commission from. I had also been warned in a dream that I was not going to be welcome at The Vineyard for long, and that ultimately, things were not going to turn out very well for the prophetic movement there either. I had only shared this dream with one of the men who was there at the ranch, and neither of us wanted to believe it. However, during that time I became convinced that the fulfillment of that dream was inevitable.

This is not to blame John, or The Vineyard, for all of the problems that were to later arise between The Vineyard and the prophetic movement. Certainly plenty of mistakes were made by both sides. I want to discuss this a little here because it is important to understand the course I have taken in building MorningStar. I am also telling this as one who was never an official member of either The Vineyard or The Kansas City Fellowship, though I was friends with and have been richly blessed by both.

The relationship between the prophetic and The Vineyard was the fulfillment of a prophetic word that Bob Jones had received. In that word there was to be a relationship between the prophetic movement that was then emerging in Kansas City and a movement that was strong in compassion and worship that was located about forty miles south of Los Angeles. This movement was later identified as The Vineyard. Also, Paul Cain had received a revelation about a Christian leader who was called to do some extraordinary things to set the table for the last-day ministry, and John Wimber was identified as being that person Paul had waited so long to meet.

In my opinion, John was that leader, and he did do what he was called to do to set the table for some of the extraordinary events that are even now taking place. It is also my opinion that the worst mistake that the prophetic movement made in relation to John and The Vineyard was trying to turn the prophesied friendship and "cross pollinate" these two movements into a marriage. It was a great relationship until it was taken too far. In one conference, John Wimber declared publicly that the prophetic had "saved The Vineyard." Later it was said publicly that the prophetic had almost killed The Vineyard. I think both statements were true. I was glad that the prophetic people did not retaliate publicly with how The Vineyard had almost killed them, but that was also true. It was a wonderful friendship that turned into a terrible marriage.

The prophetic did help The Vineyard for a short period of time, and as I was privy to the situation, I think that it may have been accurate that the prophetic was even used to save The Vineyard, if not from destruction, at least from a lot of unnecessary devastation. I think The Vineyard also did the same for the prophetic.

For a time, John, Carol, and other Vineyard leaders were a great help to the young, immature, prophetic movement that was aligned with the Kansas City Fellowship (there are other prophetic movements that were not a part of this story). If the two movements could have just thanked each other after the first year, agreeing to remain friends, having interchange and a close relationship, but not get married, I think many things could have been a lot different. This is a hard lesson for many to learn. Just because there is unity, it does not mean that there has to be a union.

I'm sure that there are some on both sides of this issue that would disagree with my conclusions of why things went sour in this relationship, and there probably are many factors that I do not know about. However, the situation did end badly. Even so, though it is certainly not true with all, there seems to still be a remarkable amount of grace, love, and affection for those who were on both sides of this.

I for one feel the pain that came from this situation was well worth the gain that also came from it. I also feel that the lessons from what happened can spare many others from making the same mistakes, and that is why I want to be forthright in sharing my views concerning them. I am not doing this to expose anyone or blame or justify anyone. I want to only share what I think may save others from making similar mistakes.

It should also be kept in mind that there are always at least two sides to a story, and sometimes many, and they can all be very different. Just because they are different does not mean that either is wrong. Often such things are like the proverbial blind men examining the elephant. One thought that it was like a tree because he examined its leg. One thought that it was like a giant leaf because he examined its ear. The other thought that it was like a giant rope because he examined its tail, and so forth. Most issues, such as the relationship between The Vineyard and the prophetic, are complex, multi-faceted issues. So please keep in mind that what I share here is only one perspective of the whole.

I have felt for many years that the old shepherding movement, the Maranatha movement, and The Vineyard movement, have potentially produced some of the greatest leaders in our times. However, many of these are still wounded people, and if their wounds are not healed, they will almost certainly be disqualified from their ultimate purposes. Unhealed wounds are a primary reason why church history is filled with so many great men and women of God who accomplished so much for the gospel, only to die in infamy.

Some of the potentially greatest men and women of God have not even been in consistent fellowship in a church for many years. These must be recovered. We need them. Others are leading churches, but their own unhealed wounds are keeping unnecessary divisions stirred up in the body of Christ. Others fell into sin and feel that they are forever disqualified from ministry. However, just like King David after his fall, some of their greatest contributions to the gospel can be ahead of them.

For every one of these who is healed and placed back in the army of God, the whole church will be greatly strengthened. This whole story is about redemption, and the Lord wants to redeem everything that happens to us so that we can truly say, **"And we know that God causes all things to work together for good to those who love God, to those who are called according to His purpose"** (Romans 8:28).

CHAPTER NINE
EARTHQUAKES AND CONFERENCES

Jack Deere had become the associate pastor to John Wimber at The Anaheim Vineyard Fellowship. On my very first visit there, I had a dream that I perceived to be prophetic. It was a straightforward dream that indicated that John Wimber was going to become enraged at the prophetic, and that the prophetic would be driven out of The Vineyard. At the time I was given this dream, there was almost a euphoria between both The Vineyard and the prophetic. I knew that no one would believe my dream at that time, and I did not even want to believe it. Like we do with many such revelations, I thought it revealed a strategy of the enemy that we should pray to be thwarted.

Now I am going to back up a bit to share about the introduction of the prophetic to The Vineyard. It began in such a way that it is remarkable that John was ever open to it, which reveals a lot about the grace and openness to the Lord that John had. Everyone who really knows Bob Jones knows that he gets some very strange revelations at times, but they are more than just remarkable in how they tend to apply to situations. John Wimber's first introduction to Bob was when Bob asked him at a Vineyard Conference if he had considered the fairy tale, *Jack and the Beanstalk*. John's reply was, "Not since I was about eight." He looked at Bob as if he was talking to a nut case and probably thought he was. Later, when John heard some of the accounts of Bob's prophetic ministry and determined that he wanted to meet him, he was shocked to discover that he was the one who had asked him about *Jack and the Beanstalk*.

Paul Cain's introduction to John Wimber was a little more dramatic. Jack Deere, Mike Bickle, and I had asked John to meet with Paul, and though he agreed to do it, he did not seem too enthusiastic about it. Then John heard the account of Paul's recent visit to the Kansas City Fellowship and became intrigued. Paul had called Mike to tell him that he needed to come to Kansas City to help heal the "staff infection." Paul had discerned the problems in Mike's staff. Mike agreed that Paul should come, but was surprised to hear Paul say that when he came it would snow, and snow would remain on the ground for the time that he was there as a sign from the Lord that their sins would be washed away. Mike asked Paul if he meant literal snow. He did. This was remarkable because not only was no snow forecasted, but it was too late in the spring for snow, even in Kansas City. When Paul came, it snowed just like he said, and the ground remained covered until he departed.

Hearing this, John Wimber became interested in Paul, so he asked Mike for Paul's phone number. John called Paul, and then called Mike back, asking him to repeat the "snow story." Mike told him again. When Mike finished he said, "You get snow, but I'm getting an earthquake!"

John related how Paul told him that he would indeed come to meet with him in Anaheim, and the day that he came, there would be an earthquake in Southern California as a sign that the Lord had arranged the meeting. John asked him when he was coming, and Paul's response was that he would come whenever John asked him to come. In disbelief, John asked if that meant he could choose the day that the earthquake hit. "That's right," Paul said, adding that on the day that he left there would be another stronger earthquake somewhere else in the world as a testimony that what the Lord was going to do through their meeting was going to be felt around the world.

The day that Paul came to meet with John, an earthquake hit at 3:33 a.m., which was centered under Pasadena. The Scripture that John had been given for this meeting was Jeremiah 33:3, **"Call to Me, and I will answer you, and I will tell you great and mighty things, which you do not know."** The drama around this meeting was understandably quite high. By then we were a little used to seeing spectacular things, but there was a destiny on this relationship between Paul and John that seemed exceptional. Much of this was because of an old promise that the Lord had given Paul of which he was convinced this was the beginning.

Paul had been told that he was going to be joined to a Christian leader who the Lord would use to help begin the restoration of the prophetic ministry to the church. Over the years, Paul had visited more than thirty Christian leaders, and he was watching for the signs that God had given him to recognize this leader. Paul was convinced that John was the one. It was hard for any of us to argue with an earthquake, so we were all thrilled that Paul's search had finally come to an end.

Paul and John connected immediately. Almost everyone who meets Paul is quickly won over by his graciousness and humor, which is at times corny, but often truly supernatural. John loved the Holy Spirit and every manifestation of the Spirit, and Paul was unquestionably moved by the Spirit. On the day that Paul left Anaheim, there was another significant earthquake in Armenia that got the world's attention, just as he had prophesied.

The Spiritual Warfare Conference

John asked Paul to come to his upcoming Spiritual Warfare Conference, and Paul agreed. Paul was not specifically asked to speak, but just to attend, as were Jack, Mike, and myself. We were just beginning to know The Vineyard. Even so, our expectations were higher than I could ever remember them being for a conference. Jack, Mike, and I were convinced that Paul would end up speaking and that something spectacular would happen that would make a true beginning for the restoration of the prophetic to the church. Like many of our expectations, what took place was quite different from what we were expecting, which was a good pattern for things to come, though none of us probably understood it at the time.

John spoke the first night of the conference. It was about as dry a message as I could ever remember hearing. It seemed that John just read from his notes, and though the content was good, there just did not seem to be any life in it. After the meeting, we were sitting with John in his office and he looked over at Mike, Jack, and I and asked us how we thought it went. We told him the truth, which he already knew. "Paul's supposed to be speaking, isn't he?" John asked. We agreed. John agreed to let Paul speak the next night.

I think we all felt the meeting that night could go down as a significant one in church history. When the time came, we were all on the front row. Paul began with a few dry jokes that weren't very funny. Even so, since everyone at the conference had heard the story about John and Paul's meeting and the earthquake, they were cheering him on, even laughing at his jokes as if they had never heard anything that hilarious. That was to be the highlight of the meeting. Paul's message was worse than John's! He, too, just read from his notes and his notes weren't nearly as good. We came expecting to be filled and left drained and confused.

I'll never forget the look that John gave us in his office that night after the meeting. "What happened?" There was no disguising that this had been one of the driest meetings any of us had ever sat through. Even worse, several thousand people, who had paid quite a bit to attend this conference, had been through two days of some of the worst meetings any of us had ever experienced. Still, we begged John to give Paul another chance. To our surprise, John agreed to do it. Whether he just did not want to speak again himself or felt that he now had nothing to lose, he asked Paul to speak again. John was obviously doing this more out of a resignation than out of vision. We were all feeling pretty defeated.

Even so, feeling it or not, this was an act of faith on John's part. Conferences were a lifeblood for his ministry at the time, and this one was turning out to be one of the worst. Even so, I think John simply wanted to do the Lord's will more than he wanted a great conference. John used to tell us that "faith is spelled r-i-s-k," and he was willing to take supreme risks to see the Lord move in great ways. This is probably why John and Carol Wimber and The Vineyard movement experienced some of the greatest miracles in the last quarter of the twentieth century.

I felt for all of the people who had taken their time and spent so much money to come to such a bad conference, and I was concerned for John who was risking so much. However, it seemed that something much more serious was at stake as Mike, Jack, and I drove to meet with Paul at his hotel room after he spoke. We thought we had a clear word from the Lord that this was going to be the beginning of something significant. On the way, we half-jokingly and half-seriously talked about two of us trying to distract Paul while the other one stole his notes so that he wouldn't try to just read them again.

Paul was expecting us, and to my surprise, mentioned right away that we could not have his notes. He continued as if he had heard our conversation on the way over. He reminded us that the Lord often made him look as weak and inadequate as he really was before He could use him in a great way. This was so that the people would not look to him but to the Lord. He seemed quite confident that the next night would be different. Jack, Mike, and I were encouraged, but I think all of us had substantially lowered our expectations for the next night. I was just hoping for a good enough meeting so that it would not be a total loss.

The next night we sat on the front row again and noticed right away that Paul looked different. He was confident—his words were clear and his message sharp. Even his jokes were funny. In the middle of the meeting, it suddenly seemed like Paul was wrapped in light. I felt the fear of the Lord come over me like I had not felt in a long time. Something extraordinary was going to happen.

Paul had been telling us stories about the healing revival days of the 1950s when they used to hope that someone would die in their meetings so that they could raise them from the dead. The spiritual energy that I was feeling was so intense that I started thinking that I could not live in it long. Then I started thinking that Paul was about to get his wish—I was going to drop dead in the meeting so I could be raised from the dead! I prayed that nothing would go wrong. I think I would have run out of the meeting, but I couldn't move.

A cameraman moved up beside me to get a closer shot at Paul, and it seemed like something came out from Paul like a cloud that enveloped the camera. Paul then had a few breathtaking words of knowledge that were on a higher level than most of us had ever heard before. The meeting ended in this spectacular crescendo and we were out of there! I was glad just to be alive.

After the meeting, we learned that a surge of power had gone through the camera that had been beside me and burned it up. The engineer who examined it estimated that it would take several thousand amps to fry it like that. Because the camera was operating on batteries, this kind of surge was not possible. We then discovered that the phone system throughout the building, consisting of about sixty phones, also had a surge of power go through them that had blown the fuses in all of them. This would certainly be expensive, but John and Carol both seemed happy just to have witnessed such a powerful move of the Spirit. In one night, the conference had gone from one of the worst ever to one of the greatest.

There was also a message in this surge of power. These power surges coming from Paul were a phenomenon that has followed him from time to time. The Lord doesn't do things like that unless there is a message in it. We felt that this one was pretty obvious—our systems were not prepared to handle the kind of power that the Lord was releasing—especially the communications system. I believe that this same problem still exists.

The Spiritual Warfare Conference in Anaheim that year was no doubt recorded in heaven as the beginning of something significant. Years later, it continues to unfold. Also, like the Spiritual Warfare Conference, we would be severely tested and stretched before the Lord would do what we were expecting. John's willingness to risk so much to give the Lord room to move as He wanted would be a continual requirement to see the glory of God. Over and over we would be asked to seemingly risk everything. We would have to endure looking foolish and empty many times, being reminded every time that this was our true state without the Lord.

We would also experience the glory and power of the Lord to the point where many times we would wonder if we could live through it. Just one of these experiences was worth it all. We are not here to build ministries, but to prepare the way for the Lord to do what He wants to do. Every time He appears, all of the works of man seem silly and presumptuous. When we stand before His judgment seat on that great day, we will not be commended or judged by the kind of ministry we built, but by how obedient we were. Our goal must always be to do His will. One minute in His manifest presence is worth more than all of our labors on this earth, so we are trying to keep all of our work focused on preparing a place for Him to dwell.

Because those attending the Spiritual Warfare Conference were from all over the world, news of what had taken place there went around the world. It marked the end of Paul Cain's wilderness years and the beginning of a year in which we witnessed some of the most intense activity of the Holy Spirit that we had seen up until that time. It also began some of the worst persecution that any of us had yet witnessed.

CHAPTER TEN
GERMANY

Mike Bickle had often mentioned to me the burden he carried for Germany. I had also remembered Art Katz once telling me that he considered Germany one of the most important nations on earth. This had really made me curious since Art was Jewish. When Paul Cain and Mike asked me to go with them to speak at conferences in Berlin and Nuremberg, I was extremely interested and agreed. I had met the pastor who was hosting us in Nuremberg at Bob Jones' house one day, and though he seemed young to be taking on such a venture, his faith and zeal for the Lord were impressive. I was excited about this trip, but I had no idea how life-changing it would be.

COLONEL EUGENE BIRD

When we arrived in Berlin, Paul Cain asked me to join him for dinner with an old friend at "the Prime Minister's table" at the Kempinski Hotel. I was intrigued, and from the first minute I met Colonel Eugene Bird, I knew I had met a prince of God.

Colonel Bird is a piece of both American and German history. He had been one of our elite fighters in WWII, and it was his company that had seized the Remagen Bridge before the Germans could blow it up, allowing the Allies to cross the Rhine River, possibly saving them months in their conquest of Germany. Colonel Bird also had been one of the first American soldiers into Berlin after its capture by the Soviets.

Colonel Bird told me how he had hated the Germans so much in that war that he prayed every day to be kept alive so he could kill more of them. With all of the horrendous destruction of WWII, when Bird entered Berlin, the devastation he saw challenged him. The Soviets had possibly lost more men taking that one city than America lost in all of WWII, including the war against Japan. There seemed no way to even estimate how many Germans had died in Berlin. The city was so devastated that the Allied commanders felt that it would be impossible to rebuild, estimating that it would take more than thirty years with hundreds of boxcars a day just to move the rubble out. With almost all of the German men having died defending the city, there seemed to be only women left, and they had been terribly ravaged by the Soviet troops who had been let loose on them for weeks. The commanders concluded that they should move the survivors to other German cities and let Berlin lie in ruins.

The survivors, almost all women, refused to go. They said they would rebuild their city, and the next morning there were long lines of them picking up the rubble, brick by brick. Bird was so moved by their resolve that all of his hatred for the Germans instantly turned into respect and and eventually grew into love. He then prayed and asked the Lord to somehow use him to help them rebuild their nation. Bird's prayer was answered when he was made the U.S. Commander of the Spandau Prison, which housed the Nazi war criminals after the Nuremberg Trial.

At this post for seven years, Bird spent as much time as he could interviewing the Nazi leaders. He also wrote the book, *The Loneliest Man in the World,* about Rudolf Hess, Hitler's Vice Chancellor, and the one who wrote the Nazi bible with Hitler, *Mein Kampf* (My Struggle). This book became an international bestseller for seven years, and Bird had gotten Hess to initial each page of the manuscript to verify its authenticity (this book was recently republished under the title, *Prisoner Number Seven*).

Bird had also been instrumental in leading some of these Nazi leaders to the Lord while they were in prison, including Albert Speer, Baldur von Schirach (founder of the Hitler Youth), and Rudolf Hess. His stories about them and their conversions were some of the most interesting I had ever heard. I also felt that Colonel Bird had a spiritual insight about what had happened in Germany that had led to the Nazi takeover, which was critical for us to understand.

One of my great interests in going to Germany on this trip was having been shown that the same demonic powers and principalities which had taken over Germany in the 1930s, had been seeking inroads into the United States to do the same thing. At the time, this seemed far-fetched, but I had been shown it so clearly that I knew it was true. I was shown America taking a big swing to the left, and then an economic meltdown would cause an overreaction that would cause it to swing to the extreme right. This would result in a terrible persecution of the Jews in America and a militarization of America that exceeded anything before. That was the end of what I was shown, but I was also told that this could be prevented. Because of this, I was on a mission to understand what had happened in Germany, and Colonel Bird was probably the greatest resource in the world.

The Knights of Malta

While we were having dinner with Colonel Bird, I mentioned to him the history I had discovered about an ancient order of knights called "The Order of St. John," or "the Knights of Malta." Because of their famous battle on the Island of Malta, they prevented one of the most powerful armies of Islam from their conquest of Europe by defeating them. Bird said that he not only had heard of this Order, but that he had recently been knighted and was a member. He also said that my books had become popular in the Order and that I had also been recommended to be knighted. He told me the name of an Austrian Baron who had recommended me and that he would soon be contacting me about it.

I thought this was interesting, but I was not as interested in joining this Order as I was in meeting some of them and learning more about their history, which I had found to be one of the most compelling of any history I had studied. I was especially interested because of what we had been shown earlier about how communism was going to fall, but the remnants of it would join with Islamic extremists to become a far more dangerous force to the world than communism had been. This little band of Christian knights in the Middle Ages had stood almost alone against the most powerful armies of Islam. After enduring some of the most terrible onslaughts and sieges in history, they had stood their ground and turned back the hordes of Islam. I felt that we would need this same kind of courage to stand against some of the spiritual powers in the times to come. I had been shown that by honoring our fathers and mothers, spiritual and natural, we could receive an impartation.

I wanted to write the history of the Knights of Malta in order to honor them. I felt that Christians would one day have to understand many of the principles that are taught by this history, and that we would have to do this in order to receive an impartation of their courage for standing against some of the same enemies. However, learning that they still existed, and that I had been recommended to be knighted by them, did intrigue me. I thought this might be an even more powerful way to get this impartation of courage to stand against some of the greatest threats of our time. However, I also wondered if they were still boldly Christian, as I had no interest in joining anything that was not and that did not have a devotion to further the kingdom. This story would unfold in a most interesting way over the next couple of years.

The Tour

The next day Colonel Bird took Paul Cain, Reed Grafke, and myself on a tour of Berlin that was the most interesting tour I had ever had been on. I was later told that when Colonel Bird gave the same tour to *CBS News* years before, it was the only documentary they had ever run without editing a single minute. Bird had also gone on to be a guest on the show *60 Minutes* more than anyone else. He was truly a walking national treasure, a library of information who had more insight about the Nazis and WWII than I had ever heard or read before.

I will not likely forget standing on Hitler's bunker with Colonel Bird, Paul, and Reed as Bird pointed out things and described events there. A neo-Nazi who was also there giving his own tours would contradict everything Bird said. I'm sure the young man had no idea that he was talking to someone who was by then recognized as one of the foremost authorities on Nazi Germany, but Colonel Bird was so gracious to this young man, never once getting impatient, or taking offense, that I was astonished. I could tell he was thinking of this young man's soul, and he did his best to sow a few gospel seeds in him before we left.

The Berlin Conference

I could have spent weeks with Colonel Bird, but the conference began at the Südstern Church the next day. This had been the Kaiser's church, which still had his gold guilded throne in it, and Peter Dippel's congregation had been able to buy it for one dollar after the war. Of course, this was under the condition that it be restored and kept as a tourist attraction, but a dollar. I told Peter I would give him a $1.50 for it right then. It was stunningly beautiful, with balconies and able to seat at least two thousand people right in the heart of Berlin.

During the conference, I saw Colonel Bird get up and leave each night and wondered where he was going. I discovered that he was going to the crowds outside who had not been able to get in and he was ministering to them, especially trying to find unbelievers he could lead to the Lord.

Colonel Bird's house is a historic building in Germany and was the only building left that had been designed by Albert Speer. Some consider him the greatest architect ever, and believe his genius as the Nazi minister of armaments kept the war going in Germany for two years longer than it could have otherwise. He designed "The Bird House" for him while he was a prisoner at Spandau and Colonel Bird was the American Commandant. It will likely become a museum, but the greatest treasures he had were the stacks of gospel tracks that he thought were especially effective.

Colonel Bird was of such stature in Germany that he could call a press conference and every station would cover it, or he could walk into the Prime Minister's office to meet with him without an appointment. Over the years as I was with him in Berlin, he would be out on the streets almost every night witnessing to individuals about the love of God and His Son, Jesus. I want to write a book about Colonel Bird, and I think it could be one of the most interesting histories I could write. One of the most special things that I loved about him was his love for God and his unwavering devotion to seeking the salvation of those who did not know Him.

We had a good conference there, but not exceptional. The best thing about this conference had been getting to know Mahesh Chavda better, who had joined us, and a big Texan named Bobby Conner, who came because the Lord had told him to connect with us. I had also gotten to know Wolfhard Margies, who had been called "the second coming of Sigmund Freud," but had left his brilliant career in psychiatry to become the pastor of one of the largest and most dynamic churches in Germany. I spoke in this church on Sunday and spent some time with him at his home afterward. Just a few weeks before, many from his congregation, along with the people from the Südstern Church, had been seen all over the world sitting on top of the Berlin Wall singing worship songs as it was being torn down.

This was truly a remarkable time in Berlin, and indeed all of Germany, as the whole world was changing, and the changes seemed centered right where we were. Berlin has become one of my favorite cities in the world. It has no doubt been a center of huge world events since Napoleon marched from Berlin for his invasion of Russia in 1812. The sense of history is great, but there also remains a great sense of destiny. I have no doubt that great world events will yet take place there.

NUREMBERG

On the train ride from Berlin to Nuremberg, we were all in the same car in a compartment with chairs facing each other so that it was easy to talk. It was a great time with Paul, Mike, Mahesh, and the others, but I was really fascinated by Bobby Conner, and got him to tell about the things he had been experiencing prophetically. He had been a Southern Baptist Pastor for more than twenty years, and then the Holy Spirit fell on him and he started living a remarkable supernatural life of miracles and prophetic revelation.

It was also stunning riding across what had been Communist East Germany a few months before. It was deeply depressing, with no color anywhere, and most of the buildings still had bullet holes that had not been repaired from WWII. I had experienced some communist countries before, but that day I was touched like never before by how evil communism was and how it stripped people of their very humanity and made them automatons. There was possibly no greater contrast anywhere between communism and democracy than could be seen in East and West Germany. Though it was very hard to see, I wanted the impression branded in my memory, and it was.

By just writing about this now, I feel the same thing that I did then. I can also feel the encroachment of this same spirit into the fabric of America, and at times, it seems too much to bear to see the way our nation is going. I've been seeking to understand how the same evil is trying to take root in America for more than twenty years. It will not come as a Nazi again, but it will somehow be a combination of Nazism, Communism, and Islamic extremism. I know it can be stopped from taking America, but only if the church in America awakens, and at this writing she is still sleeping pretty soundly, but may be beginning to stir just a little.

America will soon be in the greatest battle ever for her existence, and this foreboding is something I cannot help but to speak and write about. I know it finds its way into almost every message I give. Since I was first shown what would seek to take over America, and indeed the world, I have felt a calling to sound an alarm, to understand and articulate it, seeking the anointing and empowering of God to wake-up those who can stop it, even if it is but a tiny band that the Lord will use like the ancient Knights of Malta were used in their time. Who knows, maybe the Lord has kept this Order alive for more than nine hundred years to use it again. Their force is attacking some of the greatest leaders, both present and future, that I have ever met. Even if it is but the smallest appendage of the body of Christ, the Lord can defeat the most powerful hordes of hell with His little finger, and He may choose to do so.

As the train pulled into Nuremberg, I could feel that we had really stirred up something spiritually. Nuremberg had been Hitler's "spiritual capital," and where he had held some of his largest rallies. He had a large parade ground there, overseen by an expansive structure designed as a replica of "Satan's throne," which the Germans had excavated from the biblical city of Pergamon and had built a museum for in Berlin. The Pergamon Museum survived the war and is still in Berlin, having this "Satan's throne," which was an altar to Baal on which they performed human sacrifices. **"And to the angel of the church in Pergamum write: The One who has the sharp two-edged sword says this: 'I know where you dwell, where Satan's throne is" (see Revelation 2:12-13).** This museum also has the excavated gates of Babylon and other biblical artifacts.

We were going to host possibly the largest Christian gathering in Germany since the war on the very grounds where Hitler had reviewed some of his largest Nazi rallies. We were told that the leader of the Lutheran Church in Germany had come out publicly against our conference, warning all Lutherans to stay away. This may have been some of the best advertising we got, because hundreds of Lutheran pastors came among thousands of people. The excitement in the city was electric, and so was the spiritual realm, on both sides. We were to nightly experience demonic and angelic visitations. This was a spiritual battle more intense than I had ever seen, but the conference was spectacular, and one of the most powerful I can remember.

THE BRIEFCASE

The day before the conference started in Nuremberg, I had been standing in the lobby of the hotel talking to Bobby Conner when a man walked in, who obviously recognized me and started coming over. As he got closer, Reed Grafke recognized him and called out his name, which was the man

Colonel Bird said had recommended me to be knighted by the Order of St. John. Though Colonel Bird had assured me that this Order was strictly a Christian Order and did not have any secrets or weirdness, I still did not know him that well at the time. I felt that such a mysterious Order could very easily have become quite weird over nine hundred years, and I wanted something from the Lord about it before I could consider being a part of it. So I stopped this Austrian baron before he could say anything and asked Bobby Conner to "give me a read out" on him.

This was not entirely spontaneous, because when this man walked in, I saw Bobby look at him and could tell that he was getting some kind of prophetic revelation about him. This baron looked stunned, maybe because of what I had just asked Bobby to do, and he stood there speechless. Bobby said that when he came in he had a vision of him giving a unique briefcase to a man named Kurt Waldheim, which Bobby badly mispronounced, but was at that time the Prime Minister of Austria. The baron's mouth dropped. Before he could say anything, Bobby went on to describe the briefcase and even what was in it. This baron was visibly shaken, and said he had never experienced anything like this before. He had just had a custom-made briefcase like the one Bobby described for his friend, the Prime Minister, and had just come to Nuremberg after giving it to him in Vienna. He knew that no one could have known this, and he was instantly convinced of the prophetic ministry.

This baron immediately contacted Prime Minister Waldheim and told him what had happened. Somehow Kurt Waldheim had told an emissary for Saddam Hussein about this, who had told Saddam, who was very intrigued by such prophetic gifts. Saddam ended up sending some of his people to the conference in Nuremberg to check it out, and they became convinced of the prophetic ministry. Many of Saddam's top leaders were Christians, including his deputy, Tariq Aziz. I cannot get into all of the details of this here because it would almost require another book, but this ultimately resulted in Paul Cain twice visiting Saddam Hussein at one of his palaces in Iraq. Saddam believed Paul to be a true prophet and treated him like a head of state.

No one gets to be a dictator by being a nice guy. Saddam Hussein was no doubt one of the more ruthless dictators of recent times. However, like Nebuchadnezzar, whom Saddam considered himself to be the second coming of, God did speak to him and used him in some ways. Saddam saw himself like Nebuchadnezzar as being destined to destroy Israel like the ancient king of Babylon had done. Paul used his visits to try to turn Saddam from this course but to no avail. It was because of this intent that America would later have to destroy Saddam and his regime. As I observed what happened through this series of events, and other similar ones, I became convinced that the Lord may always try to turn world leaders from making huge tragic mistakes, even if they rarely listen to or heed the warnings.

The prophetic conference in Nuremberg had been big news in Germany. It was one of the most powerful that we were a part of in those early days, and it did have an impact not only in Germany, but across much of Europe. I was shown a large front-page article about the conference the day after it was over, and was told that there was not a single negative word in it (I could not read German). I thought this was unusual until later we heard that Paul Cain may have called out every journalist in the conference by a word of knowledge, and they had become so convinced of the reality of the prophetic that they did not dare write negatively about it. Though I had to leave and was not there for the visit, I was told that the head of the Lutheran Church had come to publicly apologize for coming out against the conference and had offered to fill the largest stadiums in Germany if we would come back. I was not sure he really had the clout to do this since his own people had obviously not listened to him to stay away from this conference, but I appreciated the gesture.

CHAPTER ELEVEN
THE VINEYARD

After the Spiritual Warfare Conference in Anaheim, The Vineyard movement was very much on my personal radarscope. During this time, I spent much more effort trying to serve The Vineyard than I did building MorningStar. I began to meet and spend time with many of The Vineyard pastors and leaders and speak in many of their churches. They all seemed to be truly amazing people, and I started to feel that I was going to meet some of the greatest people in the world at each new church I visited. I don't think I was ever disappointed.

During this time, I think I received much from John and Carol Wimber and many other Vineyard leaders that we have incorporated into MorningStar. Because my parting of ways with The Vineyard was not the most positive, and what I give them credit for they might consider blame, I still have almost all positive memories of those times and The Vineyard movement, and I am very grateful to them.

Like most new movements, The Vineyard was not perfect, and there were some fundamental problems that are common with almost every movement, even those that have created great advances for the kingdom. Regrettably, some of these problems are still found in most of the more established churches and denominations, but we have to also keep in mind that the whole church is still a work in progress. The Vineyard was no doubt a work in progress, but it was sure exhilarating being a little part of it, though I was never an official part.

There were also fundamental problems in the new emerging prophetic movements, as well as the one based in Kansas City, which were likewise exciting to be a part of. These problems were different from the ones that The Vineyard was dealing with, but it seemed to be God's design to use the friendship of these two movements to help each other. Certainly this was accomplished to a large degree.

As usual, the devil intended otherwise. As is always his strategy, the devil wanted to get each one focused on the problems of the other in the spirit of accusation instead of the Holy Spirit, the Helper. The Lord allowed the devil his shot to help speed things up, and it did. Even in the early days of the melding together of these two movements, there was some tension, but I thought it was to be expected. Handled correctly, it would all get worked out. Sadly, it never really did. Even so, the experience was valuable for all who were a part of it and most did not get cynical because of it.

The Persecution Begins

I was eating breakfast with Mike Bickle at a café in Anaheim when he first brought up the persecution that was beginning against the Kansas City Fellowship (KCF) by a fellow pastor in Kansas City. There had been prophetic warnings about this attack for years, even identifying who it would come through. Even so, it had been the policy and teaching of KCF to always pray that such negative words, which represented the strategy of the enemy, would be thwarted and not come to pass. However, this one was coming to pass.

When I first received the taped message that the pastor in Kansas City had made accusing KCF of many errors, deceptions, and violations of integrity, I had a hard time believing that anyone could listen to it and not discern in even the first few minutes the spirit of jealousy and accusation that was on it. Therefore, I did not believe that it could do any real damage, but rather the opposite. I felt that if the enemy was so blatantly attacking KCF, it had to alert the truly discerning people that something of great significance was going on there. It was one of the great revelations to me of the state of the church that very few seemed to discern the spirit in which that tape was made.

Mike was speaking at a MorningStar conference that we were hosting in Atlanta when he received a thick book outlining the accusations from the pastor in Kansas City that had made the tape. I read through much of it with

Mike, and I was boiling. I knew the KCF pretty well by that time, and I felt that everything I read was in fact the exact opposite of the truth. I could not remember reading anything so full of such blatant lies. What shocked me even more was how calm Mike was about it. He told me that he knew the way he handled this was both his greatest test and his greatest opportunity. He said he knew that God gave His grace to the humble, and he read the whole book looking for anything that was even partially true so that he could humble himself and repent of it. I was amazed because he actually did see this attack as the greatest opportunity he had yet had to grow in the grace of God.

I still marvel at Mike's grace throughout that ordeal. I don't think I know of anyone who has been more falsely accused or who handled false accusations with more grace. Still, by that time, I felt that Mike needed to answer the false charges for the sakes of those who were obviously not very discerning; Mike felt otherwise. He said that if he did not defend himself that the Lord would raise up others to defend him. I resolved to be one of those who would defend both Mike and the KCF. I did not do very well at it either.

Going Too Far

As these events were unfolding, I had been a Christian for about twenty years, enough to watch how Satan would trip up those that he could not stop or he would get behind them and push them too far. I personally think this describes much of what happened next.

It was at this MorningStar conference in Atlanta that Mike also announced that KCF had joined The Vineyard. This was shocking and disheartening news to me. I felt that it was a tragic mistake that could be even more devastating to KCF than the false accusations, which were quickly being spread around the world. It was not that I had anything against The Vineyard, but I never saw KCF and The Vineyard being called to a marriage, but rather to friendship. I noted the response of a Vineyard pastor to this news when Mike announced it, "Oh no! Now you're just one of us." I too felt that KCF had somehow lost its remarkable identity.

Though I have never changed my opinion that it was a mistake for KCF to join The Vineyard, I have also never doubted that it was done for noble reasons on both sides. I think we may rarely have perfect motives, but I never saw evil intent with anyone involved in these matters. KCF was under one of the most energetic attacks of the accuser that any of us had ever witnessed. Not only that, there were mistakes being made in the handling of the prophetic which Mike felt that he needed more mature leaders to examine and help him with. Mike was a very young man to be leading a movement of such power and influence, but he was already one of the best leaders I knew, far beyond his years in wisdom and maturity. Mike looked up to John Wimber as the wisest leader that he knew who had an understanding of the supernatural gifts and power that he was having to try to pastor. Mike was not just looking for covering, or to hide behind someone from the attacks, he wanted help, which is understandable.

Though I empathized with Mike's need for help to pastor the extraordinary movement and powerfully gifted people that had been gathering at KCF, I could not shake the feeling of dread that I felt when they joined The Vineyard. I was also carrying the burden of the vision that I had been given foretelling of a coming change in John Wimber and The Vineyard, which indicated that John would ultimately turn against the prophetic. I had never shared this with Mike, though I had tried to be forthright about the potential danger whenever I could. All that I could see now was the coming of complications. Besides confusion with his growing relationships with movements outside of KCF, I also felt that because Mike was now a Vineyard pastor and was so close to John Wimber that this would threaten some of the other Vineyard pastors, bringing conflict there too. I was right. I did not consider that this might also bring division within KCF, but it did that as well.

I am sharing this because it did have far-reaching consequences that had a basic impact on the development of MorningStar. We will come back to this part of the story, but I need to back up a little to talk about this conference we were hosting in Atlanta, which was the first conference MorningStar had hosted away from our home base in Charlotte.

A large Assembly of God church had graciously offered their facilities for this conference, which we had determined to have in Atlanta because we had been shown that Atlanta was not only a spiritually strategic city for the

South, but in some ways for the world. This revelation had begun during a series of meetings for YWAM that Brent Rue and I had spoken at in Amsterdam.

PRINCIPALITIES AND STORMS

Brent was a Vineyard pastor from Lancaster, California. He and his wife, Happy, had become two of my closest friends at The Vineyard. They seemed to me to be the quintessential Vineyard leadership couple. They were evangelists, they walked in power, they loved life, and they seemed to have joy in everything they did. They loved Europe, especially Scandinavia, and they saw both YWAM and Amsterdam as strategic for reaching Europe. Since I had been shown a coming revival in Europe, I agreed to go with them on a trip that began in Amsterdam and would also go on to Sweden and Norway. Little did I know that I was not going to teach as much as learn some of the most important lessons of my life and would radically affect my understanding of unfolding world events. Please bear with me as I relate some of these because they are related to Atlanta.

I arrived at the airport in Amsterdam before sunrise and was met by a YWAM missionary who drove me to their mission base in the city. As we were approaching the city, I looked up and saw the spirit of death hovering over the city. I was a bit shaken but said nothing. At first I did not know if it was somehow related to what awaited me there, or if it was just an attempt by the enemy to intimidate me. As we approached the city, I don't think that I had ever felt such a presence of evil.

I sought the Lord in earnest, and He began to speak to me about what I had just seen over the city. He also gave me instructions to inform the YWAM missionaries of what I had seen. I was told to warn them not to try to confront this principality, or pray against it, because they did not have the authority to do this. I was told to share it with them for their own understanding so that they could get personally free of its grip over them, and this truth would begin to set them free.

In the first meeting with the YWAM missionaries, I was asked directly if I had seen anything over their city. I told them that I did, and that I would share it with them, but not for the purpose of them beginning to do warfare against it. I also told them that when I shared this information with them that great wrath would come against Amsterdam, and people would die in the city. I knew it sounded spectacular, and some present were obviously skeptical, but that night they became believers.

I had been shown that this wrath would come against the city because the light of truth begins the breaking of the power of the enemy. He hides in darkness, and therefore hates to be exposed because it begins his displacement. When he is "cast out of heaven," he comes to the earth with great wrath. That is why it is crucial for the church to be prepared before the enemy is exposed in this way. Done at the right time and in the right way, the enemy's wrath can be thwarted. I knew that the church in Amsterdam was not ready for this, but there was a bigger picture, and I was walking in obedience to do what I did.

When I shared that the principality over the city was the spirit of death, I saw some of the missionaries jump, almost like an electrical shock had hit them. Some began sharing about the way that an uncharacteristic fear of death had been creeping into their lives and controlling them. This was unusual because they had been fearless missionaries, often risking their lives to preach the gospel in some of the most hostile places in the world, such as Afghanistan and other Middle Eastern countries. This simple truth began to set them free immediately. I again warned them not to try to do warfare against that spirit over Amsterdam because it was not time to displace it, but just to focus on getting free themselves.

That night a storm that was not forecasted came in from the North Sea that was said to be stronger than any storm in more than a century. Dozens died in Amsterdam, and many more died on the British Isles. The Lord protected us and the YWAM missionaries, except for two who had not heeded my warning to not do warfare against the spirit of death. They went home and immediately began to pray against that spirit, and they were both almost killed that night. They survived, but both had serious injuries.

As we sat in the meeting that night, with hurricane force winds pounding the building, I began to think that I was certainly in way over my head. My "comfort" from the Lord was my acknowledgment that indeed I was over my head and always would be, but His grace would be sufficient. He said that if I ever started feeling adequate for what He called me to do that I would be a very dangerous person.

That night I looked around at the YWAM missionaries. Even though many of them claimed to have been tied up by this fear of death, they seemed to me to be some of the most fearless people I had ever met. I felt that there were some in that room who would actually calm storms worse than the one raging outside. This began a great love and respect in me for YWAM. I began to feel it had a great future that night, even brighter than its history, which was already remarkable.

Gates of Hell

We all knew if the power of this spirit of death was to be broken off of the city, it would be important to understand the open door that allowed it to come in. We all speculated about how Amsterdam had been used by the Nazis to export many Jews to the death camps, but I had the feeling that this was more ancient than that. Then one day when I was walking toward the Centrum Train Station, the Spirit spoke to me, saying, "South Africa was a Dutch colony." I was completely unaware of this fact and had for some reason thought that South Africa was a British colony. When it was confirmed to me that it was indeed a Dutch colony, I knew that this was a basic key to understanding the spirit of death. Even so, there were obviously some more missing pieces to this puzzle. Certainly we prophesy in part and know in part, and I knew I only had a very little piece of this one.

Not long after this, Francis Frangipane and I were speaking at a conference together in Cleveland, Ohio.

This was another key strategic city that we both felt would one day host a church of extraordinary unity and power. Since we were in the habit of asking the Lord to give us understanding of the evil principalities and powers over a place that we ministered to so that we could speak truth to help break their power, we were shown that death and racism were primary strongholds over Cleveland. This was surprising to both of us. Then the Lord spoke and said simply, "Racism empowers the spirit of death."

While in Amsterdam, I was also given a vision of four large spiritual powers that were called "world rulers," and racism was one of them. Racism had large centers of power located in cities. I saw four of these, which were Amsterdam, Cape Town, Jerusalem, and Atlanta. There may be more, but these were the four I was shown. These were all spiritually connected as if they were on the same power grid somehow. I knew that if the power over any one of these was broken, it would substantially weaken the others as well.

Francis and I began to see how racism was the root of almost every war and conflict in the world at the time, and for many wars in history, such as World War II and our own Civil War. War is one of the most efficient ways for the spirit of death to work its evil. Cleveland is where Francis and I first began to speak out against racism and where we both began to develop our understanding of this ultimate enemy that the whole world will have to face in the end.

Wimber's Warfare

John and The Vineyard were constantly being attacked from all sides for just about everything. Almost all of these attacks came from Christians. If the external attacks slackened even a little, it seemed that something major would arise within The Vineyard. How he did as good as he did under this constant pressure was a marvel to me, and I hated it when I felt called to confront him or warn him about something else that would happen. Therefore, I was always surprised when he asked me to do so much with him. One day, when he asked me to go to a meeting with him about something very important, I was honored but curious as to why.

It was a personal meeting with a close friend in which John wanted to confront some concerns he had about spiritual warfare. I think he just wanted me to hear what he had to say since the news about Amsterdam and other incidents were being talked about so much then.

Peter Wagner was a very close friend of John's, and I know he loved and respected Peter a great deal. However, John was beginning to have issues with Peter's views on spiritual warfare. As I sat through this meeting with John and one of Peter's associates, I think it was the first time I became aware of John's concerns about this. I was keen to hear the views of each one, but I honestly left the meeting agreeing with both of them.

I shared John's concerns about immature or misguided Christians being endangered by getting into fights they were not called to have, and some had paid a dear price for this. I was willing to admit that I had taken some unnecessary shots because of this. However, I did not think we could disregard the incredible fruit of strategic level spiritual warfare, especially as they were obviously a factor at the root of some of the great revivals of our times, such as those in Africa and South and Central America.

During this meeting, I did feel concerned that John was not at least open to considering the other side of this issue. He basically said that there was no place for such strategic level warfare, but all that he could see us being called to do as in Scripture was to cast out demons. Certainly a case could be made for that, but you could make one for there being more as well. The evidence that there was more to this was substantial. If something is not that clear in Scripture, then we have to judge the fruit. There was a huge amount of good fruit from strategic level warfare, and I could only see a few cases where the fruit seemed to be bad, and there seemed to be a good explanation for them. I left this meeting a bit disconcerted, feeling this could be the beginning of a division that was really unnecessary. It was, and it would ultimately divide John and me as well. It also seems to me to be one of the devil's ultimate victories when he can get us to divide over how to fight him.

THE HOLINESS OF GOD AND GOLF

Even though there were storms brewing, I was greatly blessed and influenced by this time I had with John, The Vineyard, and the many friends I made there. One of the highlights of this time was introducing Leonard Ravenhill to Mike Bickle and then to John Wimber.

Leonard had been one of Mike's heroes for years, and he agreed to speak to the Kansas City Fellowship. I got up early to go to the KCF building in Grandview, Missouri, and I ran into Bob Jones. He told me about a prophetic dream he had of going to "Satan's trophy room," where Satan kept his most valued trophies. Two that Bob had seen there were "David's harp," which represented worship, and the other was a standard on which was written, "The holiness of God." Bob said that he was then taken to a golf course, and several of us were playing golf. He said one hit the driver, another hit the next shot, and I did the putting. He said that when I putted the ball, it hit the flag and went in. Then he looked at the flag and it was the standard he had seen in Satan's trophy room, "The holiness of God." Bob also said that this had something to do with me going to Scotland. Bob knew nothing about golf, but I knew that Scotland was where golf was invented. Bob then said that he was also told that I needed to play golf—that I was a workaholic and I needed this for recreation.

I then heard that Leonard had come into the building so I went to see him. When I sat down in front of him, he did something I loved to see him do. He really was a prophet with a long boney finger that he would shake at you when he spoke sometimes. He started shaking his finger at me like that, indicating he had something very important to tell me. He said that he knew the church was going to recover true holiness in Scotland and that I had to go to

Scotland. This really got my attention since Bob had just said this a few minutes before.

Then Leonard really surprised me by telling me that I needed to play golf. I took this even more seriously then and bought a set of clubs and started playing. Next I was told that the Lord would add the time to my life that I spent playing golf. There is no doubt in my mind that this has happened because I do tend to be a workaholic, and golf relaxes me. I also think it has enabled me to be far more productive. When I start going brain-dead in the afternoon, I can go out and walk nine holes and come back fresh enough to work for hours more.

I'm sure other forms of recreation have been good for others. Recreation means re-creation. We need some of this in our lives, and it can be a holy thing.

Leonard was a big hit at KCF, and being with such zealous young Christians greatly renewed his vision, too. However, I never expected Leonard to hit it off with John Wimber, but we decided to introduce them. They hit it off like long lost brothers and became inseparable for a time. John asked Leonard to come speak to the church there, and I thought this would be a good one to sell tickets to because I could not see it coming off without a conflict. Leonard was very old-school Pentecostal, and many debated whether Christians in California even knew what the word *holy* meant. John even preached on Sunday morning in his gym shorts sometimes, and you could see kids in skimpy bikinis in the audience.

When Leonard started speaking, I was watching both him and the congregation. Leonard did not talk about holiness that I remember, but I do remember seeing girls at least trying to cover up a bit, and then I watched some going to their knees, crying and repenting. Then about half the people were flat on their faces on the floor, wailing. I was shocked. I was even more shocked when they begged for Leonard to come back. John decided to host a conference called "Holiness to the Lord," and had Leonard as his main speaker. It was a huge hit, though it did of course offend some.

When John did this with Leonard, my respect for John went even higher. He knew Leonard could be a bit legalistic, but he also knew how badly they needed to hear about character and living holy before the Lord. He was determined to have those who followed his ministry receive what they needed.

CHAPTER TWELVE

MorningStar
Conferences

In 1990, we hosted our first MorningStar Conference at Lifespring Church in Pineville, North Carolina, a suburb of Charlotte. Paul Cain and Bobby Conner were the main speakers, as well as myself. Leonard Jones had put together a worship team from some of our local friends, and Ricky Skaggs, who was one of the top country music singers at the time, came and jumped in as well. We had a great time, but nothing historic occured, except for the fact that it was our first. However, after it was over, I had a taste of the fear of the Lord like I had not experienced before.

I knew Paul Cain had received a number of prophetic words for individuals during the conference. At each meeting, we waited for him to give them, but he didn't, most of the time because he said he was not feeling up to it. The night before the last day of the conference, I had a dream about men from Florida who had come for a word from the Lord, and they did not get it, and left empty. I was shown that this word would have given them crucial direction for their lives. Then I was shown the anger of the Lord for them not getting the word that He had sent them there to get.

I had never witnessed the anger of the Lord like that, and I was deeply shaken by it. I shared it with Paul, imploring him to give the words that he had that day. He did not. As we were leaving the parking lot, a couple of guys from Florida came up to the car just to meet us, and I knew they were the ones in my dream. I knew Paul had to give them the words he had for them, but he wouldn't do it. Not only was I gripped by the fear of the Lord, but it left me feeling like a failure and also that the conference had been a failure.

I realize many people were blessed at the conference, and some even said it was a spiritual highlight for them, but it was not close to what it could have been. It did accomplish putting the fear of the Lord in me—that the calling of God's people together is serious business, and we never want to do it unless we are going to give them our very best.

Atlanta

I shared previously about how I had been shown that Atlanta was one of the four key cities in the world for breaking the power of racism. It was for this reason that I also began to pray earnestly for Atlanta. As I prayed, I saw more about the spirit of racism and the spirit of death. I saw how the Lord had used Martin Luther King, Sr. and Jr., and why they had been based in Atlanta. They truly had been given a portion of the spirit of John the Baptist to prepare the way for the Lord and to begin eroding the power of this ultimate enemy—racism.

While sitting in my hotel room in Atlanta, I picked up the *Guide to Atlanta*. When I opened it, my eyes fell on the words, "The battle for Atlanta decided the fate of the South." This was in reference to the Civil War battle for Atlanta, but I knew that it was just as true of the coming spiritual civil war of which I was beginning to get glimpses.

While I was contemplating all that was happening with Mike Bickle and KCF, I was also starting to see pieces of something that was much bigger than all of our ministries. I began to see how all of these issues were related. It would take me years and the addition of quite a few more pieces to begin to understand it all. I knew that I would be linked with many others for other purposes, but when the battle of racism began to rage in the church, Mike, Francis, and I would be together, as well as Bob Jones and Bobby Conner, who also had been given much insight into this while we were in Nuremberg.

The Atlanta conference was another big learning experience for us in how to host conferences. At the time, accusations were beginning to come that we were trying to organize the church like the Shepherding Movement had done in the 1970s. I think anyone who got a glimpse behind-the-scenes and saw how disorganized we really were would have instantly known there was no danger of that!

To give you an example of how disorganized we were, when we were praying with some of the Atlanta pastors just before the first meeting of this conference, one of them asked who was leading worship. It had not even occurred to us that we needed a worship team. I asked if anyone present played an instrument. Several did, and there were some present from a worship team in a Vineyard church. I told them to put together something for the conference, and in a short time they had a worship team.

Even though we were so disorganized, the kind of leadership this team displayed is the kind I love to see. Identify the problem, evaluate the resources available, confront it the best you can with what you have, and go forward with decisiveness. The worship at that conference was, especially under the circumstances, remarkable. Worship was such a fundamental part of the culture at The Vineyard that they were "ready in season or out of season" to worship.

Mike, Francis, and I fired the shots that we hoped would begin mobilizing the churches in Atlanta to rise up in the unity that would be needed to fulfill their important destiny. They didn't. There seemed to be grace from the Lord in that conference, but any conference can only accomplish so much. We prayed for Atlanta, took one day off, and the following day hosted the second MorningStar conference on the road in Arlington, Texas.

Texas

Arlington is in the middle of the Dallas/Fort Worth Metroplex, which we perceived to be another great strategic place in the Spirit. Never could I have imagined two more different conferences than the one in Atlanta and the one there. After they were over, they seemed to be one in the Spirit. In them we did address different issues, but they were linked much more than we understood at the time. There was a third that would begin the linking together of the three primary foundations of the calling of MorningStar. All of the side issues were a part of our training. We thought that we were calling together all of these people to teach them some things, but the Lord had brought them together to teach us.

One main contrast with this conference was that it was actually organized, but with no thanks to us. James Robison had loaned us his sound system, and Jeanne Rogers who led worship for James' crusades had agreed to lead worship for us. T.D. Hall and Dudley Hall, who had become great friends and who I still consider two of the greatest men of God I've known, as well as having impeccable Texas character, were anchors for this conference. So guess what principality we addressed in Texas? PRIDE.

I still can't believe how stupid we were after having had the daylights beat out of us so many times by principalities and "world rulers," that we were going after probably the biggest one of all. Somehow we got away with it, and lived to do it again. However, some of the great churches and ministries in the region were chewed up pretty well after we left, which could have been because we stirred up something without having a clear strategy for fighting through to victory.

Our main purpose for conferences at the time was to just initiate some things that the local churches and believers could continue. However, we did not have enough understanding ourselves on strategies for this to result in serious breakthroughs and ultimate victories. It has taken us twenty more years to see some of these things, but I do think these conferences did have accomplishments, just nowhere near what we were hoping for.

Also, Texas may be known somewhat for its pride, but it has a lot to be proud of. I personally love the culture in Texas and greatly appreciate a place where the men can be men and the women are ladies. I may like the geography in other places better, but if I had to choose another place to live other than where I do, especially for raising my children, Texas would be it.

One reason for this is when I was sitting in a friend's office in Dallas. I had a vision of a large heart beating in the middle of the city. When I inquired about what this was, I was told that it was the Lord's heart, and He was going to reveal His heart there. He also said that He was "gentle and humble of heart," and that when He revealed His heart there, Texas would become known for its humility.

Texas is also a place that I would try to visit at least once a year just to get my vision and hope for America recharged. Certainly there has been an erosion of morality and some integrity there, like everywhere else in America, but you just know when you're in Texas that there are some things they are never going to compromise, and like at the

Alamo, they may just die to a man before they compromise. Texas has provided a lot of salt and light for America, and I may often poke fun at Texas and Texans, but I do this with those I have the most affection and respect for. I for one am very thankful for Texas.

The Vision

Speaking at other people's conferences was much easier than hosting our own. We had survived our first few, but it had stretched out the team to the point where I thought each conference probably drained us of six to twelve weeks of extra energy. Of course, Steve, Angie, and the others we had added to our team did most of the work, but it was a huge task planning them, coordinating speakers, and so forth. Of course, each conference became a little easier as we learned how to do them, but they were still a major undertaking, and I would have been fine not to do any more. Then I received a vision in which I was shown the strategy of the Lord for them.

I was shown that the Lord was going to use conferences in the times to come like He had used the feasts in Jerusalem for Israel. Israel was commanded to gather three times a year in Jerusalem to worship the Lord and feast and fellowship with one another. If they had not done this, they would have separated into their different tribes and lost their common vision as a nation. I saw how the different denominations and movements were like the different tribes of Israel, all having a unique purpose and calling, but they also needed to receive and maintain their vision for the whole body of Christ, which conferences would help them to do.

Now almost every church hosts conferences, and most are contributing to the necessary interchange and cross-pollination that is needed in the body of Christ for it to be healthy. Just as any flock of sheep will get weaker with each generation if it is not allowed to crossbreed with other flocks, Christians, movements, or denominations that stay isolated from the rest of the body of Christ will get weaker with each generation.

EPILOGUE

This book is a brief history to explain some of the people and major events that influenced the foundation of MorningStar. Two remarkable years were 1988 and 1989, and most of what I covered in this first volume took place during those years. However, there were many other key events and people who we began relationships with at that time, but their real impact with us was later, so I have saved their stories for the next volume.

Even though 1988 and 1989 were such remarkable and supernatural years, some of the most extraordinary supernatural encounters, and the real jelling of MorningStar into what it has become, began after this. In those two years, I gave myself mostly to helping other ministries, and it was at the end of this period that I was able to give more focused attention to building MorningStar. However, MorningStar has always been about having a vision for and building up the whole body of Christ, which is basic to our nature. Our nature is also the result of the input of many others, which we value greatly, and I hope you have been able to perceive this in this first volume.

During those first two years, I was traveling far more than I was at home, and Steve and Angie Thompson, along with Leonard Jones, were doing much of the work to organize MorningStar into what it was to become. Steve, being drawn to the prophetic and equipping others in it, started drawing a small group together to equip and release into this ministry. Robin McMillan, a friend who I had first met in the 1970s, also joined in helping to establish what we called "the School of the Spirit" or SOS meetings. Leonard, who I considered one of the greatest musicians I had ever met, joined our team to develop the worship aspect of the ministry. The story of the development of our SOS meetings is a key factor in understanding who we are as a ministry now as well as in the next phase. Therefore, I felt it needed to be the beginning of the next volume of this history.

As I write this in 2009, it has been about twenty years since many of these events and experiences occurred. I can now see their impact on MorningStar and in me even more. Our goal for MorningStar has never been to be big, but rather to stay focused on simply doing the will of the Lord and helping to equip His church for these times. We have continually emphasized that we are but a small part of the whole body. MorningStar is still not very big compared to other ministries, but we have made quite a large footprint in the body of Christ for the last two decades and are poised for this to greatly increase. We have counted as many as sixty-five nations and virtually every major denomination being represented in a single MorningStar conference. We have also had grace to reach across barriers and boundaries that we value highly. We believe that our true success will not be in how big or influential we become, but by how the whole body of Christ grows in power and influence with the Lord and with men.

Therefore, our goal as a ministry is not to be written in human history books, but to be in God's history books which are "The Books of Life." As I write this book, MorningStar is in the first stages of going through a major metamorphosis, a radical change, which will help position us for the next twenty years. When we stop changing, we start dying, and the fact that we are now going through such a transformation is encouraging, indicating that the Lord is not through with us yet. Even though change is coming, the core values and principles that were sown into our fabric from the beginning will continue with us and will always be a part of who we are if we remain on track with the purposes of the Lord.

One of the reasons why I felt I needed to write this history is because we are spiritually about to cross our Jordan River and start possessing our Promised Land. This is true of MorningStar, but it is also true of the body of Christ. Before Moses let Israel cross over, he called all of the tribes together to repeat the whole law and history. This is where we get the Book of Deuteronomy. We are now reviewing our history and core values for the same reason—to consider where we have come from, to remember and be thankful for the great works of the Lord, and to reconnect with our basic purpose and values before entering into a much bigger land and purpose.

Reflection for the purpose of strengthening the foundations, the cords that bind us together in a purpose of the Lord, is needed at times. Even so, we must always keep in mind that the past no longer exists, that we live in the present, and must do so with a vision for the future. This book is written for the purpose of understanding our past so that we can better understand the present and our future purpose, which we must go on to. The story of our history does get more exciting, but the best is yet to be experienced—it is the future.